John Moore
True Countryman

by David Cole

Books by the same author:

The Detective & the Doctor: A Murder Casebook. (with P.R.Acland)

Geoffrey Prime: The Imperfect Spy

A Writer's Guide to Police Organisation and Crime Investigation and Detection.

Cover and Title page pictures by Abigail Cole

First published in 2007
by
Blacksmith Publishing
The Paddock, Lower Moor,
Pershore, Worcs. WR10 2PA

Printed by Aldine Print Ltd., Six Ways Trading Estate,
Barnards Green, Malvern, Worcs. WR14 1NB

ISBN No. 978-0-9543585-1-8

Contents

List of Illustrations

Books by John Moore

Author

Dixon's Cubs	Published - 1930
Dear Lovers	1931
Tramping Through Wales	1931
King Carnival	1932
English Comedy	1932
The Walls are Down	1933
The Welsh Marches	1933
Countrymen	1934
The New Forest	1935
Overture Beginners	1936
The Cotswolds	1937
Clouds of Glory	1938
The Countryman's England	1939
A Walk Through Surrey	1939
Life & Letters of Edward Thomas	1939
Wits End	1942
The Fleet Air Arm	1943
Escort Carrier	1944
Portrait of Elmbury	1945
Brensham Village	1946
The Blue Field	1948
Dance & Skylark	1951
Midsummer Meadow	1953
Tiger-Tiger	1953
The White Sparrow	1954
The Season of the Year	1954
Come Rain, Come Shine	1956
September Moon	1957

Jungle Girl 1958
Man and Bird and Beast 1959
You English Words 1961
The Year of the Pigeons 1963
The Waters Under the Earth 1965
Among the Quiet Folk... 1967

Plays

The Elizabethans 1963
The White Sparrow 1964

Co-editor

The Book of the Fly Rod (with H.T. Sheringham) 1931
The Angler's Weekend Book (with E. Taverner) 1935

Editor

Whitbread Craftsmen 1948
The Boys' Country Book... 1955
Best Fishing Stories 1965

Acknowledgements

I owe a debt of gratitude to a number of people who have willingly helped with my research. I am particularly indebted to John Moore's wife, Lucile and Daphne, his sister, with whom I spent enjoyable hours listening to their frank reminiscences: regrettably, neither of them lived to read my efforts.

The project would not have reached publication without the knowledge and assistance of John Shakles, Chairman of The John Moore Society, who made the author's archive available to me and gave freely of his time. Robin Stayt, the Moore family genealogist, guided me through the intricacies of an extensive dynasty and I received further expert assistance from Simon Lawton, curator of the John Moore Countryside Museum. Simon, Mike Renouf and John Shakles were kind enough to offer constructive comment on my original draft – to the extent that it bears little resemblance to the finished product!

My thanks are also due to the following for providing answers to my many questions: Norman Rosser, the archivist of Malvern College; Dala Dickins and Diana Prance, former secretaries; Paul Humphreys (sadly no longer with us), BBC talks producer; Grenville Simons, a master at The Elms, Colwall; Harold Peer, a fellow serviceman with John Moore at Royal Naval Air Stations, *Ford* and *Piarco*; Ernest Hughes, retired employee of Moore & Sons: and Robert Moreland, a relative of John Wilton Haines.

Valuable information was researched for me by archivists at Marlborough College; Charterhouse and Shrewsbury Schools; Royal Navy & Fleet Air Arm Record Offices; Royal Navy History Branch and the Department of Research, RAF Record Office. My friend since schooldays, Michael Hurley, used his extensive experience to unravel several seemingly impenetrable mysteries surrounding John Moore's correspondence.

Extracts and quotations are published by kind permission of: The John Moore Society; *Country Life Annual, 1964* (Country Life); *My Life & Times* (Society of Authors as Literary Representatives of the estate of Compton Mackenzie); *Wavy Navy* (Eric Dobby Publishing); Dame Barbara Cartland (Cartland Promotions); *Country Column* (S.Dyson, editor, *Birmingham Mail*); *The Book of the Fly Rod* (Derrydale Press); *Homes & Gardens* (Southbank Publishing Company). The quotation by Richard Church on *September Moon* is reproduced by permission of Pollinger Limited and the proprietor.

Every effort has been made to trace holders of copyright. I very much regret any inadvertent omissions, but these can be rectified in any future edition.

David Cole

Foreword

I have always been interested in the countryside and books on the subject. It was in the 1970's that I discovered the writing of John Moore when my work took me to the villages around Bredon Hill, about which he wrote so vividly in the years after the Second World War.

The first John Moore book that I read was *September Moon,* set in the hop fields around Ledbury, swiftly followed by *Portrait of Elmbury, Brensham Village* and *The Blue Field.* As my appetite for more brought me to his, by then, obscure pre-war books and the discovery of articles and journalism, I began to realise that there was far more to this author than an engaging storyteller about a forgotten way of life.

Sir Compton Mackenzie had described his death as a tragedy for the English countryside. Moore was a humanitarian, naturalist and conservationist. Rural England owes much to his foresight in campaigning for its protection, and his beloved birthplace, Tewkesbury, should remain forever indebted for the battle he fought to preserve much of its architectural heritage.

Since the formation of the John Moore Society in 1988 we have been all too well aware that the full story of this remarkable man's life has never been told. David Cole's biography is therefore welcome and we are pleased to support it in recommending it as a comprehensive study of a complex, courageous character, who is recognised as Gloucestershire's favourite son of the 20th century.

John Shakles, Chairman.
John Moore Society.

Introduction

Researching the life of John Moore has given me an opportunity to revisit the places of my own early years. I grew up among people he knew, roamed the same fields and hillsides, fished the same rivers and followed the foxhounds. Only a few miles separated our homes and he was a familiar figure throughout my childhood.

I first remember him as a wartime naval officer, striding, or rather loping in his strange, distinctive gait, along Tewkesbury High Street in full uniform. My mother told me he was a famous author, and it was a fact that he had written several books, although at that time his name did not travel much further than our native Gloucestershire. He mocked those early works when he became better known. 'They are all out of print,' he said, 'and I hope they remain so.'

He did himself an injustice. *Dixon's Cubs* his first book, published in 1930, is one of his best; literary critics acclaimed *The Countryman's England* which appeared a little later, and his only attempt at biography, *The Life and Letters of Edward Thomas* is a work of scholarship.

Service in the Fleet Air Arm interrupted his writing career, and he did not become widely known until a well-received anecdotal piece about life in rural Gloucestershire between the two World Wars appeared in 1945. *Portrait of Elmbury* drew heavily on his personal experiences and revealed Moore as an authentic chronicler of country life with a light, readable style.

He came back to Tewkesbury with a beautiful Australian bride, who settled his somewhat mercurial temperament, and having survived enough adventures to last a lifetime, he became content to spend the remainder of his days among the familiar faces and landscapes of his native heath. He wrote prodigiously for the next twenty years, becoming both defender and advocate of the rural way of life, fighting for its preservation and campaigning against despoliation. Moore's post-war books reflect those causes, are as relevant today as when they first appeared, and in being so earn him a considerable following of grateful countrymen, conservationists and naturalists.

This reputation, however, should not give an impression of a narrow-minded zealot; Moore was a man of many interests and particularly a lover of fun. He led a full and active life that is best summarised in his own words:

> 'I know a man who has taken part, at some time or another, in almost every sport and pastime; he's never been really good at any of them, but he's sailed, climbed, flown, fished, bird watched, bug hunted, botanised, collected this and that, taught himself a little about this and that, read a great deal about this and that, and enjoyed himself so much that he hasn't the slightest regret that none of his boyhood ambitions have been achieved ... to play cricket for the county ... to win a Grand National ... and of course become the world's greatest living expert of Hawk-moths, Wild Geese, Orchids, or whatever it was that had tickled his fancy and aroused his special interest at any given time. Instead of all this, he became an incorrigible dabbler, but expert in absolutely nothing – I am that man.' (1)

Chapter 1

The Early Years – 1907-23

'My own relations were bourgeois and ordinary ... country doctors, lawyers and auctioneers ... They had lived in and about Elmbury for so long, that they seemed to have proprietary rights in the place.' (1)

The elderly man, seated behind a vast desk, posed a perfectly reasonable question: 'But what are you going to do?' Tom Moore's nephew, shifting uneasily from one foot to another, stammered a reply that met with something resembling an explosion. 'A writer, that's a hobby my boy, not a profession.'

Thus did John Moore announce his intention to abandon life as an articled auctioneer, leaving behind the security of the family firm to pursue a dream. He anticipated resistance and, to give him courage, kept his hand firmly on a cheque in his trouser pocket. The £100 advance from a publishing house had given him the incentive to take the step that his mother and uncle were sure would lead to penury, and as things transpired over the following decade, they were right.

That version of his departure from Moore & Sons, Auctioneers and Estate Managers of Tewkesbury, in April 1931, was the one John Moore always told in later years, but, as with all good storytellers, the truth was somewhat different. For some time he had earned pocket money from writing magazine articles and poetry, putting far more effort into them than he ever devoted to his employment. He yearned for the life of a writer and the riches he believed would surely follow, to allow an extravagant lifestyle among the smart county set and hunting fraternity. His first novel, *Dixon's Cubs* had already been in the bookshops for a year and a second was on the point of publication when he made the fateful decision. He harboured no fears for his future. *Dixon's Cubs* sold reasonably well; he had good contacts in the publishing world, particularly the sporting press, and was engaged to be married. He viewed the world through rose-tinted spectacles and nothing could subdue a positive belief in his ability to secure fame and fortune. In subsequent years, however, he had cause to reflect upon the sage advice of his elders who had urged him to establish himself financially before embarking upon the life of an aesthete. The fortune did not materialise and the road towards success proved long and arduous.

Moore did not come from a literary family. When he was born, on 10 November 1907, his parents would no doubt have thought that their first-born would, in all probability, become a doctor or lawyer. They would almost certainly have dismissed the possibility that he would follow his father as an auctioneer, because Cecil Moore was the junior partner to his brother, and Tom's son would join the small family firm on leaving school.

The Moores were an old and influential north Gloucestershire family. They originated from a Worcester tanner of the early eighteenth century, whose son Humphrey moved to Tewkesbury to pursue the same trade. Subsequently, two virile brothers of the following generation were to provide the nucleus of a dynasty: William and George Moore sired eleven sons between them and these eventually followed a number of diverse occupations. Some became traditional tradesmen – maltsters, merchants, tanners and auctioneers – and others, with the benefit of better education, entered the learned professions.

William was a wine merchant, but his son Benjamin traded in wool, livestock and property from premises at 46 High Street, Tewkesbury, and it was from there that the business of auctioneer and estate management evolved. A franchise to conduct the ancient chartered livestock markets at both Upton-on-Severn and Tewkesbury added to the family's prosperity. In 1836, Benjamin's brother Charles set himself up as a solicitor in offices further along the street and was appointed Her Majesty's Coroner four years later – a position that remained in the family for more than a hundred years. Another brother established the local newspaper in 1858 and it was at about that time that several members of the family entered local politics.

George Moore qualified as a surgeon, practising in London's best teaching hospitals, before returning to care for the community around the small Cotswold market town of Moreton-in-Marsh, and to combine his duties with a passion for fox-hunting. Dr Moore had the good fortune to become personal physician and companion to Samuel Warneford, a wealthy clergyman and benefactor to the city of Oxford, who eventually bequeathed him a large house and substantial capital. New-found wealth enabled George to engage assistants, while he indulged in the chase and firmly established himself in Cotswold folklore:

> 'Going on his doctor's rounds in a gig [he] encountered one morning a very aggrieved prize-fighter, pacing furiously up and down beside a famous landmark known as the Four-Shires stone. When he asked, the large and murmurous [*sic*] crowd what the matter was [he] learned they were very angry and disappointed because the prizefighter's opponent had taken fright and failed to turn up. "I have a busy morning ... but if someone will hold my horse I shall be delighted to give the gentleman a fight ..." They fought with bare fists and my great-grandfather did so much damage to the prize-fighter's face that he had to stitch it up for him. He is said to have demanded his fee ... then wiped his hands and went on to the confinements and the measles ...' [2]

George retired after the death of his first wife, leaving his son John, to continue the practice. John shared his father's passion for fox-hunting and married a local girl with similar interests. They were fearless riders and rode out at least three days each week with the North Cotswold, Heythrop and Warwickshire hounds.

Mrs Moore's addiction to hunting was the reason for her refusal to bear a large family and she only produced two daughters, Eliza Georgina (Ina) and Lilian Mary (Molly). The girls were born into a life of middle-class privilege and educated by a succession of resident governesses before attending Cheltenham Ladies' College. Ina was seventeen-and-a-half when she enrolled in 1890, and described her single school year as the unhappiest of her life. She was quite unprepared for a lack of privacy in a dormitory and the petty discipline of an authoritarian regime:

> 'I always remember my last day. With some apprehension, I answered a summons to the Principal's room a couple of hours before the final bell. I had prepared for my departure by daring to put on my two small gold wrist chains. Jewellery was strictly forbidden. "Ina", said Miss Beale, very severely, "remove those bangles – they will impede your writing." Thereafter I foreswore that any daughter of mine would never be subjected to such treatment and humiliation.' (3)

Thereafter Ina was reluctant to leave the bosom of her family, and at the turn of the century approached thirty years of age still a spinster. Her life revolved around the management of Warneford House and endless social engagements. She had a fine, professionally trained, singing voice and was in great demand for after-dinner entertainment and musical soirees. Test matches at Lords, Henley Regatta, Wimbledon and Ascot featured on her annual calendar and she was a frequent guest at London houses of the nobility.

In June 1902 came the first indications of romance. Cecil Moore of Tewkesbury, a second cousin and considered a confirmed bachelor at the age of forty-three, drew unwelcome attention to his status by appointing a sister as official consort during his mayoral year. An aunt, Dr John's sister Blanche, contrived a meeting between Cecil and Ina over afternoon tea at her spacious home in The Crescent at Tewkesbury. Aunt Paddy, a name earned for a volatile temperament, was accustomed to getting her own way, but for once, her scheming failed. Polite conversation between the cousins did not immediately lead to a fatal attraction. Two years later, however, Ina's situation suddenly changed. Her father died only months into retirement and there was little money in his estate. His widow and daughters moved to much smaller accommodation after the necessary disposal of Warneford House, denying them the servants and trappings of their previous lifestyle. Aunt Paddy took this as another opportunity. It was fortuitous that at that very time Cecil was negotiating the purchase of the grand Tudor House in Tewkesbury's main street, which was in need of complete renovation and a woman's touch to oversee the internal refurbishment. Paddy invited Ina to stay, on the pretence that a change of scenery would help sooth her grief, and Cecil appeared at dinner on the first evening.

Different circumstances changed everything. The strong-featured, impeccably mannered young woman possessed all the qualities required of a chatelaine, and she was equally attracted to Cecil's diffidence and quiet confidence. Within days she completed a round of polite vetting by all her suitor's extended family and had much to discuss with her mother on returning to Moreton. Within weeks, Cecil asked for her hand in marriage. On 12 May 1905, she told her diary: 'The happiest day of my life – Cecil proposed.'

Less than a year after her father's death, Ina prepared to leave the high Cotswolds.

The loveliest house in Elmbury, known as Tudor House, looked out across a wide main street upon the filthiest slum … (4)

Following a brief engagement, Cecil and Ina were married in Tewkesbury Abbey on the first day of July 1905. After a short honeymoon in Scarborough, they returned to live temporarily at The Uplands, a large rented house on Mythe Hill overlooking the town, until Tudor House was ready for occupation. Cecil returned to business and Ina settled to life as a married woman. She was accustomed to domestic management and engaged sufficient resident staff to run her household, while also supervising the interior design and furnishing of Tudor House. A cook, lady's maid and general servant, all recruited for an annual expenditure of £38, allowed her sufficient leisure to receive relatives and friends every weekday afternoon, and the couple frequently entertained clients and associates at dinner. Ina sang in the Abbey choir, received daily Communion and in quiet moments indulged her love of literature.

Tudor House became a much more extensive and costly project than Cecil had anticipated, and when Ina miscarried after eleven months of marriage, a combination of losing her baby and worry about financial commitments affected her enormously. She remained in her room for three weeks, never again to regain any confidence when faced with adversity, and John's uneventful birth eighteen months later acted as a trigger for behaviour that tried the patience of everyone in the household. It was not exceptional for her to summon a doctor to see her baby three times a day, and from her diary entries, it was clearly an ongoing neurosis of detrimental consequence to the development of both John and his younger sister.

The failure of Cecil's health before the family moved to Tudor House compounded Ina's anxieties. John was less than a year old when, taken ill during a family holiday, his father entered hospital a month later for the removal of a tumour. It was six months before he was well enough to return to work, and worry about his financial commitments further impeded full recovery. The family vacated The Uplands and moved to smaller, rented accommodation near Tewkesbury Abbey, where Daphne was born in May 1910. Four months later, five years after their marriage, Cecil and Ina finally occupied Tudor House.

The timber-framed mansion remains as a significant landmark at the north-eastern end of the main street. It is a fine example of Tewkesbury's original architectural splendour. Constructed of timber in 1546 and named firstly The Old House, it has undergone several radical transformations over the years and been used for a variety of purposes. Bricked over in the seventeenth century and then re-clad with timbering in 1897, it has served as merchant's house, a court of justice, an academy for Dissenters, civic offices and official mayoral residence. Eventually it achieved far greater prominence as the place from which a young John Moore surveyed the passing scene, and provided material for his best selling book *Portrait of Elmbury.* The Moore family were the first private residents for almost three hundred years and its foreboding interior left lasting impressions:

> 'We didn't go out much. I was always in the condition of having a cold, of having had a cold, or of being liable to catch a cold if I got wet. So Tudor House was my world; and with its winding staircases, its dark oak-panelled corridors, its numerous exciting junk rooms and attics, and its curious and delightful back garden, it provided a domain wide enough for any small boy ...' (5)

The garden was his playground; accessed from the High Street through a stone arch and flagged courtyard, it had walls of sandstone and glowing pink-orange Georgian brick when in direct sunlight.

The house was steeped in history. An enormous oak rear door bears scars from axes wielded by Jacobite rioters, and a large royal coat of arms flanked by allegorical figures identifies a former courtroom. Gloomy corridors, a priest hole and secret chamber said to have concealed Charles II after the Battle of Worcester add to the aura. John and his sister were too young to appreciate the interior finery: carved panelling and mouldings, Queen Anne and Jacobean staircases and original leaded windows. Instead, they remembered the distinctive household odours: freshly disinfected flagstone floors, steamy laundry, food cooking on kitchen ranges and a musty apple store. And from the confines of their nursery they would gaze enviously at the antics of the urchins in the slum alleyways on the opposite side of the street:

> 'This was the place where my sister and I were most often to be found, with our noses pressed close to the diamond shaped panes, gazing out with lively interest and eager anticipation at the black and gawping maw of Double Alley ...' (6)

They had no contact with those children: their mother's stifling preoccupation with illness forbade it. At The Uplands John had also been isolated from the outside world, but at Tudor House there was at least an opportunity to observe a life of contrasts, and the companionship of domestic staff to assist his emotional and social development. A favourite was Nanny Brick, engaged as his wet-nurse when he was three days old, and from whom, more than any other, he received affection. Unfortunately, he formed a close attachment to the matronly woman and adopted her broad Gloucestershire dialect, necessitating her summary dismissal when he was three years old and the arrival of a governess of more gentle birth.

Mary was well spoken, intelligent and reliable, and, furthermore, had one significant attribute that would shape the course of John's future – a deep understanding of the natural world. During daily walks in the countryside around Tewkesbury, she introduced him to the glories of nature in fields, rivers and hedgerows, stimulating his alert and retentive brain into remembering the proper Latin names of vegetation, birds, mammals and insects. She encouraged him gently to handle any living thing, and it was not long before he began to learn to read. He made rapid progress and developed an unquenchable thirst for knowledge that encouraged his parents to purchase the complete Encyclopaedia Britannica:

> 'In a dark panelled room I curled up and read volume by volume the Encyclopaedia Britannica,

picking and choosing the articles that took my fancy from Aardvark to Zymotic diseases.' (7)

His mother never considered formal schooling: convinced that he had a weak chest, she could not countenance the perils of cold classrooms and infectious pupils. Consequently there were no distractions to his obsessive reading except Elizabeth, a second governess who gave French lessons, and a local schoolmaster who took him through the Latin Primer. He received no instruction in mathematics or science, subjects of which, in later life, he always pleaded ignorance.

Elmbury was a small town ...Over it and dominating it was the huge square tower of The Abbey: the finest Norman tower, some say, in the world ... (8)

The Moore family settled into a comfortable life at Tudor House, without any comprehension of the disruptions to their lives that would occur within a few years.

Tewkesbury, for all its stinking alleys, filthy slums and grim sweatshops, was then a place of some prosperity, whose citizens lived in the shadow of a building that had given the town purpose and stability for a thousand years – the glorious Abbey church. Tewkesbury owes its very existence to the piety of a few monks. The fording places at the confluence of the Rivers Severn and Avon attracted a settlement of Benedictines in 715, and by the time of Domesday, a Saxon manor enveloped nine thousand acres radiating from the junction of three strategic thoroughfares from Gloucester, Worcester and Oxford. During a redistribution of land after the Norman Conquest, the entire estate ceded to King William's consort, Maud.

'Then there came a good soldier, Robert Fitz-Hamon, a friend and relative of William the Conqueror; he'd lead a rough-and-tumble, turbulent sort of soldier's life, he'd killed a great many people and even

> burnt a church or two in his day, and he wanted to make his peace with God before he died. He liked the situation of the monastery at the junction of the rivers, and he decided to build a great church there and dedicate it to Our Lady. It was 20 years a-building, and Robert did not see it finished before falling to a lance-wound at the siege of Falaise in Normandy. Nevertheless, in 1123, the masons laid the last stone on top of his noble tower and the job was done ... the huge and glorious tower rises above the little town; but I can't ever tell you what colour it is, because its stone takes a light from the sky and seems to change as the weather changes – I've seen it grey as a ghost on misty days, and pale primrose in the bright sun, and old-rose in the evening, and sometimes in the light of a red sunset ... I've seen it burn with a sort of inward light, as if it were afire.' (9)

For four centuries, the Abbey supported the pious oblations of a substantial monastic community, their daily needs providing employment for a larger number of lay artisans, labourers and merchants. There were mills, malthouses, tanneries, slaughterhouses, breweries, bakehouses and laundries. Farms throughout the surrounding plain annually produced a thousand head of cattle, sheep and pigs to supply the kitchens.

Tewkesbury Abbey received many large bequests from wealthy patrons in return for promises of eternal salvation, becoming in consequence one of the wealthiest religious establishments in England.

> 'The exquisite, airy, little chapels and chantries, built round the east end as memorials to the great folk who are buried there. The names of these people are the names which made England's history – the names of the Barons who made and unmade our Kings: Warwick, Beauchamp, Despencer and De Clare.' (10)

In time, Tewkesbury Abbey also claimed a place in the nation's history:

> 'Before the altar is the burial place of an English prince who was slain at Tewkesbury – Edward, Prince of Wales, son of Queen Margaret. On 4 May 1471, the Lancastrians and Yorkists, the Red Rose and the White, clashed in a great fight at (Tewkesbury). It was the decisive battle of the Wars of the Roses, and the Red Rose lost. There was a terrible slaughter in a field which is called to this day the Bloody Meadow ... The beaten army, as many as could escape, fled into the Abbey for sanctuary; and young Edward was assassinated by the victors before his mother's eyes ... By chance a purplish-red flower, called Cranesbill, grows profusely in the Bloody Meadow; at times it almost covers it; and if you look through strong glasses from the top of the hill at this patch of England's earth on a summers day you will see the dreadful stain upon it. You will see it drenched in Lancastrian blood.' (11)

The momentous battle was still fresh in minds of townsfolk when Henry VIII ordered the dissolution of monasteries in 1540. The King's men plundered the Abbey and its monastery, but citizens who lived beyond the walls defied a command to destroy the church. Commissioners negotiated a reprieve on payment of £453; the value of roof-lead and bell metal.

Further funds were not available to save the community of monks and the majority dispersed. Monastery buildings fell into disrepair and extensive agricultural holdings disposed of, in many cases to the same baronial families who had provided the Abbey with its wealth. These new masters brought new trade, together with employment opportunities, and established a wider market economy. Tewkesbury became a busy inland port, thriving from taxes imposed on cargo-in-passage and exports originating from workshops of tanners, leather workers and stocking manufacturers.

The Abbey suffered again when travelling armies passed through the town during the Civil War:

> 'Cromwell's puritans did worse things than banning the people's harmless fun – you can see what they did in the abbey to this day. They struck off the heads and arms and legs of the many beautifully carved stone figures, and anything they could describe, as a 'graven image' was the target of their haphazard hammers ... The wicked work of these barbarians did not stop there. They stripped the colour from the walls, the pillars, the roof and the chantrys, and whitewashed the whole church from floor to ceiling ... We do not know what the interior of the Abbey looked like when it was a blaze of colour ... but little bits of the original colours are left here and there, fragments of exquisite blue and shining gold.' (12)

When peace returned, Tewkesbury continued to flourish. Entrepreneurs invested their profits in elaborate buildings and earned the town a deserved reputation for fine architecture. At the other end of the scale, with land on the flood plain at a premium, a tangle of workers' cottages occupied every available space, leading inevitably to overcrowding and poor living conditions.

> 'Tudor House looked out across a wide main street upon the filthiest slum ... Few people saw anything incongruous in this, for in those days Elmbury was a higgledy-piggledy place, of incomparable beauty and incomparable squalor ... Double Alley was something to be wondered at. Respectable women drew their skirts closer about them when they passed its nauseous opening; even the doctor and priest were unwilling adventurers when summoned to visit, and policemen took care to go in pairs ... One of the most extraordinary things ... was that little children who

> lived within it would run about naked in the full light of day. This served to sharpen the impression that it was populated by fiends.' (13)

This was John Moore's hometown, but it was his good fortune that he lived in superior accommodation and within easy reach of river and open countryside.

The Warwickshire Avon falls into the Severn here and on the sides of both, for many miles back, there are the finest meadows that ever were seen. In looking over them, and beholding the endless flocks and herds, one wonders what can become of all the meat! (14)

In the course of his rural rides, William Cobbett had gazed upon the countryside around Tewkesbury from the back of a horse; but when John Moore was old enough to be aware of the same surroundings, the means of travel had developed significantly. The thirty stagecoaches that had daily passed through the town were no more, the only remaining evidence being a number of posting houses and livery stables, where some notable travellers and their horses once rested:

> 'At the Hop Pole at Tewkesbury, they stopped to dine; upon which occasion there was more bottled ale, with some more Madeira, and some Port besides; and here the case-bottle was replenished for a fourth time. Under the influence of these combined stimulants, Mr. Pickwick and Mr. Ben Allen fell asleep for thirty miles, while Bob [Sawyer] and Mr. [Sam] Weller sang duets in the dickey.' (15)

Steam power replaced horse transport and the railways spread across the land, but only a single track connected Tewkesbury to the main network. This limited facility, proving inadequate to service factories or supplement the existing navigable network, meant that industry could not develop. The result was high unemployment, more slums and a return to dependence on farming and associated trades. During this period, the Moore family became one of the few to prosper from its interest in livestock markets and estate management. The market days gave John some of his earliest memories:

> 'Wednesday was always market day: the busiest day of the week when the town came to life. Stock arrived early, running through the streets, harried by drovers and dogs. Farmers arrived later on horseback, their wives later still – fat ponies drawing floats driven by a fat wife ... and sometimes a fat pig, turkeys or geese accompanied them.
>
> 'The beasts, fat, dark with sweat, steam rising off them in thick mists; the silly sheep driven by dogs or packed like sardines under tight netting on the carts; the long rows of monstrous, fantastic pigs ... some of them so fat that they could hardly move – parodies of living creatures; wallowing, disgusting, obscene.
>
> '... the jolly crowds of farmers ... like a fragment of Merrie England come to life again. And the drovers, exceedingly sozzled towards evening. And the comical dealers ... comical because of the curious and indisputable fact, that men grow to resemble the beasts they deal in.
>
> 'Everybody knows that horsey-look of the horse-dealer. Go to a market and you will also see large bovine men; meeker bleating sheep-like men; and even little chirpy men who deal in fowls.' (16)

Licensed premises served substantial fare: a half-florin lunch listed as Market Ordinary, consisted of soup, stewed eels, beef, mutton or pork and Stilton cheese, all washed down with copious draughts of beer or porter.

> 'Many a farmer went home "market peart", and those who travelled alone were dumped in the cart and the horse found its own way. It was said that their wives put them to bed wrapped in a length of tongue!' (17)

There was, however, another aspect of market life that the young John Moore found less attractive:

> 'Porters stuck numbers on the behinds of milling, steaming, wild eyed, frightened cattle. The sticks of drovers went tat-tat-tat on the backbones of the beasts ... I can still smell the sweaty hides, feel the press of flank or shoulder as I was swept along by the panicked herd. I can see the eyes of the cattle, so brown and gentle in the fields, but in the market almost always showing the whites of terror. I remember the sense of all pervading fear.
>
> 'Bacon pigs were loaded up disgracefully by those who did not understand that if you want to move an animal the quickest way is to be both gentle and quiet. Pigs when frightened almost always begin to fight amongst themselves.
>
> 'Sheep packed so tight in the pens that you wonder on a hot day how their sides manage to heave with their desperate, frightened breathing.
>
> 'Everybody – farmer, dealer, drover, hanger-on – carries a stick, and uses it, often quite pointlessly ... by poking an animal's ribs or smacking it across the rump to emphasise an assessment or bid.' (18)

Those practices set him against his father's calling and instead he explored the livery stables and thoroughfares, discovering other excitements.

> 'Railway wagons, pulled by a team of huge horses, bore their loads of flour from Healing's Mill. The red

> flag waved, whips cracked, carters yelled, slithering horseshoes kicked up sparks, the wheels rumbled on the rails – making a fine old commotion in a town which was otherwise as quiet as the grave.
>
> 'When the fire bell sounded Nanny would scurry us along to the corner of Mill Street to watch the commotion.
>
> 'The alarm was raised by breaking a glass panel in a box to obtain the key to the front door and then ringing the bell. On hearing the call, casual fire fighters dropped whatever they were doing and rushed to the Swan Hotel for horses. Often these were at pasture at Mitton, two miles away, and the men had to run there to catch them and ride back to town. If the horses had been out all day drawing carts, they were often reluctant to forego their leisure, and catching them, particularly at night in a ten-acre field, became problematic, especially when the firemen had been in the pub beforehand.
>
> 'Often, by the time the horses were harnessed to the pump and galloped furiously through town towards the fire, it had burnt itself out. That, however, did nothing to detract from the spectacle.' (19)

The town's two rivers had an important part to play in commercial and community life. Long horse-drawn barges transported flour and hay to feed both human and horses in the industrial Midlands, and returned with coal and commodities. Pleasure boats and ferries carried passengers under the watchful gaze of hopeful anglers or idle observers.

> 'You will see them there most fine evenings, after they have had one at the Black Bear. They have strolled along to the bridge to 'see what the river is doing' – for the river does a great many things besides aimlessly swilling the sandstone buttresses, and some of these

> things concern the old men's very livelihood ... (there is) a really professional way of looking over a bridge ... leaning on the sandstone parapet worn smooth by the elbows of generations ... puffing their pipes, and occasionally, with great accuracy, spitting on a water-lily leaf ... the old men are not very talkative ... "be ruz," says the first, weightily ... "two-three inches," says the second ... "they eels'll be down tomorrow" ... These old men read the river like a book ... old Nobbler, the ferryman shoots the arches in his punt on the way home ... and the old men, having completed their rite of staring into the water hobble off back to the Black Bear.' (20)

The gentler Avon provided pleasurable days for many families:

> 'The Rowing Picnic involved preparations almost on the scale of a military expedition ... sandwiches, buns, pats of butter and little jars of jam, hard-boiled eggs, "and we mustn't forget the tea, and the kettle, of course, because tea always tastes funny out of thermoses" ... innumerable rugs, cushions, ground sheets, mackintoshes and umbrellas ... an enormous rowing-boat, a double-sculler, for it had to accommodate eight of us.
>
> 'My father and my uncle had to row this galley two miles upstream. The aunts sat beneath open parasols, we children dangled our hands in the water and tried to make it spurt up through our fingers ... my father and uncle both sweated and toiled, red-faced, nearly apoplectic.
>
> 'But at last we tied up the boat, unpacked the food, tried to boil the kettle, swatted wasps and ate. "I always think food tastes so much nicer in the open air."
>
> 'We would have liked to explore, but as soon as the picnic was over it was time to go home. The swans

> were fed with leftovers and the aunts were embarked, wrapped in rugs, and once again, my father and uncle endured their long martyrdom. Aunt Paddy sometimes rowed, "to avoid the seasickness", and no one dared to disagree. With the boat tied up at the landing stage, there was a chatter of relief, even the prim aunts felt like adventurous explorers who had returned from a dangerous journey.' (21)

An idyllic childhood came to an abrupt end with the declaration of war in 1914.

> 'All my earliest impressions are bathed in light. The Ham, where the green aftermath comes up to my knees ... across the golden river the Abbey tower is incandescent in the sunset ... as the sun sinks, the great shadow of Malvern creeps across the green.
>
> 'My father succumbed to my pleas to go fishing and took me to the Abbey Mill on that backwater that the monks had cut a thousand years before to power its massive wheel. We fished for bleak in the mill pit, with flies he taught me to catch with a dab of the hand off the sun-baked wall of the mill. Everything is warm, light, golden; and memory's trick is an apt one, for the child beside the river banks basks unknowing in the sunset of an age ... Nothing would ever be quite the same again.' (22)

During the four years of that conflict Cecil Moore died and his brother Tom, senior partner of Moore & Sons, lost two sons on the battlefields of France. The firm struggled to survive, and Ina, with two small children to support, faced an uncertain future.

'Peace on earth ended when I was seven ... the Volunteers marched out of their dark and dusty, creeper-clad Drill Hall ... Farmers' sons, tradesmen, keepers and poachers and hobbledehoys

served in Flanders for the better part of five years ... they added proud battle honours to the colours of a regiment which already possessed more than most.' (23)

On the outbreak of war, Tewkesbury mobilised a contingent of forty volunteers for the 2nd Battalion the Gloucestershire Regiment. They embarked for France led by Lieutenant Harold Moore, a trainee auctioneer, his younger brother Lionel suspending his medical studies to serve as second-in-command. Harold was killed in 1915 and Lionel almost exactly a year later. When the war ended, Tom and Ellen Moore shared their grief with the families of more than one-hundred-and-fifty men who did not return.

During the conflict Ina Moore dedicated herself to voluntary work, collecting donations of meat and produce on market days in the yard of Tudor House. Cecil auctioned them and converted proceeds to essential comforts for troops at the front. Tewkesbury found itself a strategically important holding area for troops destined for France; transit camps appeared on the outskirts and many officers found billets within the town itself. Several stayed at Tudor House and, to one in particular, John Moore would be forever indebted:

> 'Collecting butterflies and moths is the only hobby, apart from fishing, that has stayed with me. I must have begun at the age of ten, with a Brimstone caught for me by 2nd Lt Tapp, who was billeted on us. He was little more than a boy, just out of school and destined for university. He did not survive the war. Three weeks after leaving us, he lost his life at the battle of Arras ... so the Brimstone must have been an early one, tempted out of hibernation by the blink of February sun. I still think it strange that he should have troubled to catch it, and to set it so carefully on the setting board he left me when he went.' (24)

Ina gave little time to the children or other domestic responsibilities, and therefore did not anticipate the financial problems that suddenly beset the family. Tudor House exhausted Cecil's money and in April 1917 they moved back to The Uplands. The stay on the hill compensated the children for a seaside holiday that was impossible during wartime. It proved to be an eighteen-month-long vacation. They now lived in greatly reduced circumstances; staff was pruned to a minimum and Ina became involved in clearing Tudor House and supervising its alteration into rented apartments. She shouldered the majority of the burden because of Cecil's delicate health. He had never fully recovered from abdominal surgery and struggled to run Moore & Sons single-handedly during prolonged absences of his grieving brother. Keeping the financial situation between himself and Ina, he tried to carry on normally as a town councillor and magistrate and was a conscientious Special Constable and member of the Home Guard. His frail physique inevitably succumbed: doctors discovered an inoperable lung tumour and gave him only months to live. He told no one, even Ina, of the prognosis. However, by Christmas he could no longer conceal his decline, spending what time remained to him with the children, taking to an invalid chair and finally his bed. Ina took him to a Malvern nursing home when he became too ill for a resident nurse to manage, and remained with him until his death on 15 February 1918.

The Vicar of Tewkesbury, Ernest Smith, delivered a fulsome eulogy at the funeral service four days later. Mourners packed the Abbey's huge nave to remember a good man who had devoted a life to business, civic duty and charitable causes. There was much sympathy for the tall, elegant widow with a child on each hand who followed the coffin to its final resting place.

Later that afternoon Ina met two brothers-in-law in her drawing room. Executors Thomas and Neville were ill at ease. Cecil had summoned Neville shortly before his death to add a codicil to his will in which he left £100 to his dear wife 'in gratitude for her care'. There were no other monies, and from a preliminary examination of the estate Ina's future looked bleak. Tudor House carried a heavy mortgage that would have to be redeemed, and the only realisable assets were Cecil's share in Moore & Sons, and his collection of silver plate and antique furniture. Thomas purchased Cecil's share of the business for £2,375. Tudor House and another small property sold for £1,800 – a third of their probate valuation – most of the proceeds going to settle builders' accounts. Within a few years, Tudor House became a hotel.

'Shortly after this, I was sent to school, underwent certain metamorphoses, and was transformed from a pampered and coddled brat into an extremely tough little ruffian.' (25)

Ina relied solely on income generated by a £3,000 trust fund set up by her late father and felt her new situation keenly. Prospects of poverty and homelessness were in stark contrast to her upbringing as a gentlewoman and she found it difficult to ignore the furtive whisperings and sidelong glances that followed wherever she went. She left Tewkesbury, settling in a rented house in Cheltenham's Painswick Road. Her priority was to provide the children with an education now that she could no longer afford private governesses and tutors. With the assistance of relatives, she managed to find fees for a small preparatory school.

Brandon House proved an unhappy experience for ten-year-old John. Sheltered throughout childhood, he did not readily adapt to playground hurly-burly or classroom discipline, and the trauma of Cecil's death had worsened Ina's irrational attitude towards the most insignificant illness. John soon learned to exploit her neurosis and spent more time at home with coughs and snuffles than he did at school. It is unlikely that the situation would have improved had not a kindly relative by marriage taken an interest. Dr Arthur Liston, one time an assistant to his grandfather, Dr John, took the boy beneath his wing. John spent summer holidays with the Listons, learning to cast a fly with Arthur and playing cricket with cousins. However, when he returned home the same problems recurred and both Liston and

Tom Moore decided that the only solution was to separate mother and son by sending him away to school.

In the early months of 1920, an opportunity arose to overcome Ina's abhorrence of boarding education. Denis Moore, a younger cousin, was due to enrol at The Elms, an excellent preparatory school near Malvern, and the idea evolved that the pain of separation would ease for both boys if John went along at the same time. In the weeks prior to his departure, Ina wrestled with her conscience, unable to conceive that her beloved and delicate offspring could possibly survive without her personal care. Eventually, under considerable pressure, she relented after receiving offers of financial assistance and tearfully led her twelve-year-old through the school gates at the beginning of the summer term. It was a turning point in both their lives: Ina could no longer stifle her son's development and John, released from her bondage, proved surprisingly resilient and adaptable.

The Elms, established in 1614, remains one of the foremost preparatory schools in England, with an enviable reputation for educational excellence and character development. The headmaster at the time of John Moore's entry, William Parkinson Singleton, previously a master at Repton, bought the school in 1916 and developed an enlightened environment for forty boys. His wife, two assistant masters, an art mistress and matron aided him. One of those masters immediately influenced John Moore and would be immortalised in his later books.

> 'I think we all resolved that when we grew up we'd be like Mr Charlton [*sic*]: and it wasn't a bad resolution, for I've never met a man who could so beautifully walk the tightrope between the practical and theoretical and get so much pleasure out of the two kinds of life which lie on either side.' [(26)]

Churton – there is no existing record of any other name save 'Churty' – was a larger-than-life classicist who dressed eccentrically in loud check plus fours with gaily-coloured gaiters.

Rotund of build with heavy jowls, he roared like a tiger but endeared himself to pupils with unorthodox teaching that contrived to instil an understanding and love for language:

> 'In good faith he would ask the definition of a long English word and, when none was forthcoming, break it down to its Latin derivation. Every period became a lesson in either Latin or Greek.' (27)

The master's idiosyncrasies appealed to his new pupil who had been fascinated by words since the lonely nursery days when he had only books for company. John Moore's precocious facility with language, literature and his knowledge of the natural world were obvious. It was equally apparent, however, that he was less competent in other subjects and reluctant to concentrate upon anything that did not immediately seize his interest. Churton identified the deficiencies and was sufficiently sympathetic to adapt the academic timetable to suit the boy's individual requirements. Giving him freedom to roam the Malvern Hills and regard the open spaces as his classroom, the master devised a syllabus largely incorporating natural history, setting the task of scientifically recording his observations. That work survives in an unpublished Naturalist's Diary, which continued for several years beyond his time at The Elms and provides an insight into the early development of a perceptive naturalist and writer.

> 'Not far away from winter now, yet today I noticed the small gnats dancing up and down on a small stream, just as they have been doing all summer. There is, to me, something a little tragic about the lives of these tiny creatures. With the rising of the sun they emerge from the tiny pupae which have held them for so long, to first perform the necessary duty of reproduction, then to dance away their lives all through the summer day until evening falls and they die.

> 'How often in a matter of fact, casual way, do we watch the gnats dancing over the water at dusk? How many millions of tiny insects are there? The dance becomes slower ... fewer insects are dancing ... another hour to live, perhaps ... Then a few million gnats will live no longer, nay, possibly many more.
>
> Just the same happens every day – happened yesterday and the day before – will happen tomorrow ... Yet the world goes on just as usual.' (28)

He observed and faithfully recorded the mating dance of stoats, nesting birds, flight patterns of bats and life cycles of vegetation.

The staff also steered him towards classic practitioners of the written word, the prose and poetry of Virgil, Shakespeare, Shelley and Longfellow. Gradually, a more rounded character emerged in place of the wary introvert, allowing full integration into school society. He had never been happier.

> 'With my new found freedom and my awakened intelligence I began to find out more than I had ever known before ... I explored the rivers and the brooks, the field-paths and the woodlands, discovered one-by-one the villages and hamlets, made friends of poachers and foes of keepers ... Summer holidays, long and leisurely, were divided between fishing and butterfly hunting, swimming and messing about in boats ... I knew the hills like the back of my hands, by day or by night. I learned to tickle trout and to read Virgil; to swim a length under water and to enjoy English history; all about catapults, and a little about Attic Greek.' (29)

John only spent six terms at The Elms before age dictated that he should leave. He spent the ensuing summer holiday with three chums from the school, Donald Elder and Dick and Ted Stephens.

Their exploits would feature many years later in *Portrait of Elmbury,* but when the idyll ended, he moved on alone, to an establishment for which he was temperamentally unsuited.

'From the glorious free-and-easy prep school I went to a hateful public school where I found I was expected in summer to play a regimented kind of cricket instead of collecting butterflies and in winter go for compulsory runs, instead of watching birds.' (30)

Sending John Moore to Malvern College, a prestigious public school, proved a huge mistake, although it is unlikely that any other similar establishment would have been capable of catering for his free spirit. His mother no doubt added to the problem by renting accommodation in the town so that he could attend as a dayboy. John detested everything about Malvern and reverted to his old ways. During the first term he spent twenty eight days at home with questionable illnesses and on the rare occasions he attended it was to rebel against the regime.

> 'I became a sort of anarchist. On OTC field days, I deserted. I refused to play football ... instead of running I concealed myself in a chalk quarry and looked for fossils.' (31)

He would later recall only one occasion when he willingly cooperated – purely by accident:

> 'The occasion was a joint field day with the OTC of Cheltenham College ... Cheltenham had a militaristic tradition ... we didn't like Cheltenham ... in due course we deployed ... by crawling on my belly, I was able to make my escape unseen by the Sergeant Major. I had some business with a solitary oak tree which I believed to harbour a sparrow hawk's nest ... I decided to spend the day there. Before long, however, three officers on horseback appeared ... The men, who were umpires,

> dismounted for a smoke in the shade and began to discuss the relative deployment of the opposing forces. I dared hardly to breathe but sat among the branches above and listened to their assessments. At last, they rode off ... I appreciated the dramatic nature of the situation ... within fifteen minutes or so the enemy would have us at their mercy. I swung myself out of the tree and began to run downhill ... I told my tale ... I had become lost, I said, I did not mention the oak tree. Our CO despatched messengers hither and thither; at least we were now facing in the right direction ... We sliced clean through two Cheltenham companies, swung round in our tracks, and fell upon the remnants.' (32)

Throughout his time at Malvern, he remained in the reception class and when his peers moved on became isolated and increasingly introverted. Any social progress he had made at The Elms disappeared as he immersed himself in books or wandered the hills alone, and it was not until his particular talents again attracted the attention of two masters that he avoided complete failure. Housemaster Robert (Judy) Porch and an assistant, Maurice (Bingo) Banks, found a key to the workings of his seemingly impenetrable personality. Porch the authoritarian figure and a more relaxed Banks complemented each other in motivating the difficult youngster. Porch developed his interest in literature, allowing him to read whatever he wished before gradually steering him towards other classical subjects and encouraging him to write:

> 'I discovered that my form was still reading Ovid's Metamorphoses and Caesar's De Bello Gallico, which I practically knew by heart; so I decided to do no work ... I decided to give up all mathematical studies also ... but I read everything I could lay my hands on, from Kipling to Shelley, from Surtees to Keats. I read all the

> plays of Shakespeare, including Timon of Athens; the poetry of Meredith and the prose of Thomas Love Peacock, the whole of Man and Superman, and Tristram Shandy four times.' (33)

Banks, a biologist specialising in natural science, exploited the only other subject that interested the boy. Together they spent free afternoons travelling the countryside around Malvern in an open-top touring car, finding fossils and wild flowers, and watching insects, birds, and animals.

The Naturalist's Diary continued to develop and, under Porch's watchful eye, John began to write verse. His dream since the age of eight of becoming a poet received little encouragement from more earthy relatives and it was not until Porch admired the freshness and originality of his style that he was persuaded to submit a composition to the local newspaper. John Moore's only purpose in life thereafter was to see his work in print.

His first efforts were naïve and a source of personal embarrassment when he progressed to more perceptive and balanced works:

> 'I walked along by Blackmore
> And heard the foxes say
> "There's Foot and Mouth at Tirley
> And hounds won't hunt today" ... ' (34)

Porch supervised his progress and introduced him to the Empire Poetry League, where members continued to widen his horizons. In the autumn of 1923, *Poetry Magazine* published 'The Stile', an imaginative piece of prose from the pen of a sixteen-year-old youth, and a payment of 7/6d convinced him that he would make a fortune from his pen.

'I was a lanky youth ... I had an astonishing store of knowledge about a number of things which were scarcely relevant to a commercial career.' (35)

Apart from a head full of dreams, John Moore left Malvern College without any idea of how he would earn a living. His sudden departure followed an uncomfortable meeting between Ina and the headmaster. John's attendance record was disgraceful and there was little evidence that he would ever benefit from the general ethos of the College. Porch and Banks could not optimistically forecast any meaningful academic progress, so his mother agreed to withdraw him at the end of the 1923 summer term. She was bitterly disappointed, having always coveted the idea that John would follow her family's medical vocation; she now faced the reality that he had neither aptitude nor ability to do so. Instead, the nickname 'Johnny-Head-in-Air' precisely reflected his dreamy personality and fanciful notions of becoming a poet. His mother could never bring herself to criticise his indolence and after leaving Malvern he spent the summer fishing, playing cricket and writing poetry. During those two months he received £1.2.6d. for two sonnets, but gave no indication that he was prepared to find a job.

Family elders again discussed the situation. They were no longer prepared to subsidise him and Ina's resources were limited in the extreme. The possibility of a career in journalism came to nothing when John failed to complete a shorthand and typing course. Then, with some hesitation, Tom Moore came forward with an idea. At sixty-eight years of age the auctioneer was looking towards retirement, but knew that his leaving would finally sever almost two hundred years of continuous family commitment to the business. He therefore offered to article his nephew at a wage of fifteen shillings a week, with prospects of a partnership to follow. The generous offer did not find immediate favour and it took a deal of coercion from other relatives to persuade John to accept. On 5 May 1924, ten months after leaving Malvern, he began his professional training.

Chapter 2

Preserving the Dynasty – 1923-31

'I could read the New Testament in Greek and recite much of the Georgics from memory. I knew the names of most wild flowers, could recognise most butterflies and moths and tell you their life histories, knew the birds' songs, their nests and eggs, and had read the whole of Geikie's Geology. I could sometimes catch fish when wise anglers couldn't; could shoot, ride a horse, sail a boat. I had read without discrimination every novel, play, or biography I could lay hands on, and I swallowed poetry with the voracity of a sea-lion swallowing fish. My method was to obtain from the Public Library the collected works of some poet; Tennyson, Browning or Longfellow, and read the whole lot, slap through, from page one to the end ... With these qualifications I set out to become an auctioneer.' (1)

The portents for success were not good. Moore & Sons had hardly changed since 1757. Rituals were strictly observed: winter fires lit on 10 October for Tewkesbury Fair remained until May Day, whatever the weather. Refreshment was forbidden and juniors under the age of twenty-one were not allowed to smoke. The dress code was a heavy tweed suit, white shirt with stiff collar and black boots. The senior clerk attended the bank at precisely eleven o'clock, spent the next hour in the pub and was not seen after four in the afternoon, when he departed with the post. Junior employees worked in the front office behind high desks and clients did their business at a counter across the entrance door. A typist operated an ancient Underwood machine in a far corner and answered a wall-mounted trumpet telephone in the rear passageway. Uncle Tom and his partner occupied the 'back office', where the only furnishings were two desks and chairs, and an enormous steel safe securely bolted to wall and floor. The upper floors stored business documents generated by four generations, and it was in those dusty rooms that John Moore secretly pursued his ambition to become a writer. For almost seven years he endured what he termed a life of purgatory, little appreciating that the rich variety of his working life would provide the material eventually to allow him to achieve his goal.

He soon became involved in market life: armed with a glue pot and brush, he slapped labels on livestock, rabbit pens and poultry cages, and standing beside his uncle to record each sale he learned the language of an auctioneer. Afterwards, the clerks returned to chaos in an office where buyers and sellers demanded instant settlement:

> 'We spent four hours or so doing sums as quickly as bookies' clerks have to do them; 35 tegs at 63s 6d, 15 hind at 2s 11d, 19 store cattle at £9.15.6d, and so on. All the time we were taking cash, giving change, making out receipts, and even writing out the cheques for those who could sign their name, but had no "book-larnin" ... We were never allowed to go home until the books balanced ... we stayed in the office until ten and eleven at night ... and never failed to get the figure right, even though a big market in those days involved a turnover of three or four thousand pounds.' (2)

Moore & Sons sold anything connected with the rural economy and an ability to agree a valuation was an essential requirement of the profession. As part of his training John rode the countryside around Tewkesbury on horseback, accompanying his uncle in a trap drawn by a little Welsh mare. He could not have had a better tutor.

> 'My old uncle had been fifty years in the profession and he possessed "the appraising eye" to the n'th degree. He could tell you what a pig weighed,

> what a fat lamb weighed ... after a moment's glance; he'd prod a 'rick with his walking-stick, walk once round it, and say, "There's just sixteen tons". Then he'd pull a wisp out of it, sniff it and say, "Worth sixty-seven pounds". He was hardly ever wrong. He'd look at a field of standing corn and tell the owner how many bushels he'd get to the acre. He could value with equal certainty an old oak chest, a set of Worcester china, a Suffolk Punch carthorse, a mowing machine and a pedigree Hereford bull ...
>
> "The art of appraisal," he would say, "if you learn it young, is like riding a bike – you never forget how to do it ..." ' (3)

Tom's ancient clerk, Bertie Grey, had similar skills, but unlike his master, was completely unqualified:

> 'His instruments were hardly ever more accurate than his eye. "Three acres, one furlong", he would say ... and three acres and one furlong it would turn out to be. As a timber valuer, he was superb. Sixty seconds in front of a standing tree and he would estimate the cubic content of timber ... he was rarely wrong.' (4)

The wizened little man had other talents. He knew both Latin and Greek as a self-taught scholar, and could recite the works of Shakespeare from memory. On their many journeys he and John exchanged classical quotations while Tom Moore ruminated on the more practical matter of his next sale:

> 'My uncle was also a poet of a kind; of the spoken word he was himself a master. I watched him, aged 75, selling a good farm in the rich Severn Vale. Field by field, lovingly he described the farm. He had a little hour glass ... he set it up before him and watched the sand trickle through it, and while his ivory hammer was

> poised above the rostrum he spoke with the tongues of man and of angels as he extorted the beauties of that farm.' (5)

John did not take full advantage of his tutor's experience. He was an almost certain heir to the firm, but instead of concentrating upon his studies, rebelled against the routines, particularly those of office life. He reflected discontent in a poem written shortly after starting work.

The Song of Exile.

'Oh, prithee hearken, ladies gay,
I sing a song of sorrow,
For as I go my way with a slouch today
And the dawn is dark tomorrow
The road is long to Malvern town
The weary miles are many
And I sit and stare in an office chair
For to earn my needed penny

'Oh, the white road is a long road
Full fourteen miles there be
A weary road, a dusty road
Twixt Malvern town and me
And doomed am I to pine and die
Of the ennui that kills
Because of the fourteen miles that lie
Twixt me and the Malvern Hills

'No air's as good as Malvern air
That blows o'er Malvern gorses
What joy so rare as a gallop there
On one of Malvern's horses?
Oh, Malvern girls are pretty girls
And Malvern folk are clever

O'er hill and dale as Malvern ale
You'll seek such drink for ever
'Ye hills grow misty blue and grey
Upon the low horizon
On foggy days ye melt away
Dear hills I fix my eyes on
The weary exile drops his pen
He seeks not fame or knowledge
The distant blue is hiding you
Dear hills and Malvern College!' (6)

'If any earnest young student with a B.Sc. and little experience of life asks me the best way to begin the study of sociology I shall suggest at least two years in the office of an Auctioneer.' (7)

John Moore did try to settle down, but after two years became increasingly disillusioned and restless. He was convinced that he would succeed as a poet if only he could break free from his possessive mother and find some way to support himself. He did not appreciate a lifestyle that would have been the envy of most youths of a similar age, regularly leaving the office early on an old motorcycle for meetings of the Poetry League in Malvern, or as a 'Stage-Door-Johnnie' pursuing a succession of young actresses at the Festival Theatre. After all-night parties on the hills, he roared back to Tewkesbury in time for breakfast. Hunting, shooting and fishing were natural leisure pursuits for anyone following his particular calling and ample invitations were forthcoming from Uncle Tom's clients. He acquired a horse, stabling it in the rear outbuildings of his mother's house in Barton Street, and his beloved Bobs, a crossbred terrier that, he said, retrieved like a Labrador.

'There came to the little stable at the bottom of our garden a succession of the wildest, raciest, maddest horses that ever made nuisances of themselves at Boxing Day meets. First, there was a bay mare Cinders, who finally capped an eventful three

> weeks by backing me into a plate-glass shop-window one Sunday afternoon. She was followed by the loveliest black called Judy, a temperamental, highly-strung creature, who would go dancing over the tarmac whenever she saw a motor bus and who smashed up the blacksmith's shop whenever I took her to be shod. And the third of that unholy trinity was a saturnine old racehorse called Brampton.' (8)

He gained for himself an unenviable reputation for wild and undisciplined behaviour when, with other young men from wealthier families, they raced motorcycles around country lanes, caroused in village pubs and became the subject of colourful comment for determined pursuit of the fairer sex. It was a way of life he could ill afford on a clerk's salary and also horrified his prim and proper relatives. He was often contrite, but did not mend his ways, always relying on the excuse of escaping from the boredom engendered by an uninteresting job for which he had very little aptitude.

His time under articles coincided with an economic depression, and an epidemic of foot-and- mouth disease added to the problems of the severely afflicted farming industry:

> 'It passed like a blight from end to end of our green vale ... The weekly markets were closed, except for the sale of fat stock to be killed immediately; and an auctioneer's painful job was to value the affected herds for purposes of compensation. Thus, I had a grim introduction to agricultural life ... when the farmers lacked ready money, there was scarcely a man or woman (in the town) whose livelihood was not affected.' (9)

Moore witnessed at first hand the distresses of bankruptcy upon honest, hard-working families and loathed his role in sales and evictions – unhappy experiences that changed his political and religious philosophies.

> 'Really, one wondered how such a man could get into debt. But he had. Oh, yes. Right up to the neck in it! There was six weeks rent due, a bill of sale on the furniture, and no less than three firms of moneylenders were interested ... He did not seem to have a friend in the world and villagers flocked to his house to pick up such bargains as they could at a sale which was, as the auctioneer facetiously pointed out, "entirely without reserve."
>
> 'So what little furniture there was had passed out of [his] hands at absurdly low prices. Now, in a discreet corner in the bar of the village inn, a number of dealers were tossing up, and dividing the spoils over double whiskies.
>
> 'All was bustle and shouting in the thatched cottage, as the purchasers tumbled over one another in their hurry to remove their bargains. In the midst of it all [he] stood as one dazed ... A woman carrying a washstand knocked into him, and two men negotiating the narrow staircase with his mahogany chest of drawers told him, roughly, to get out of the way ... Such an inoffensive old gentleman.' (10)

His outbursts about the suffering did not endear him to the county establishment and, consequently, he became something of an embarrassment for Uncle Tom. Nevertheless, of far greater concern to his devout mother was that his experiences caused him to question his belief in Christianity.

Ernest Smith, Vicar of Tewkesbury and a family friend, could not conceive that the young man whom he had christened and prepared for confirmation would seriously embrace atheism:

> 'God has given you exceptional gifts ... do not forget the giver. Your mother has told me of your doubts about coming to Easter Communion ..I am quite

> sure you ought to come. I would not be your good friend if I did not tell you so.
>
> 'My advice is not based upon religion, but common sense. If, as you fear, Holy Communion is an empty rite – a relic of outworn past – put up with it for the love of your mother – it will give her infinite happiness ...
>
> 'A meaningless custom? Well, suppose it is only that – it means so much to the one you love best – so you should go with her ...
>
> 'If there is something to it – perhaps remembrance of a noble act of self sacrifice – is it not worth coming on that score alone? One meaning of Holy Communion is "do this in remembrance of me" and a simple desire to do what is right.' (11)

John was never dissuaded from his opinion that the church's teachings contained false hopes when set against the nature of society. He used as an example the unchristian treatment of the vicar himself:

> 'The vicar was a most generous man. Indeed the vicar's generosity amounted to a mania; he gave away everything he possessed, including large sums of money, and then innocently borrowed from moneylenders in order that he might still be able to give things away. We did not know this at the time; we merely thought he must be immensely rich ... Such benevolence inevitably led his downfall. When chased for his debts he resigned to save his Bishop embarrassment and found a small parish living far away. However, he could not escape the bailiffs and in desperation shot himself.
>
> 'Being guilty of suicide his ecclesiastical masters denied a last wish that he be interred alongside his mother in the Abbey's consecrated grounds – a betrayal I can never forgive.' (12)

'I had discovered a passionate and painful pastime of writing stories.' (13)

Throughout the seven long years of his nephew's apprenticeship, Tom Moore only tolerated his indolent attitude and lack of effort from a sense of duty to Ina. John's progress was abysmally slow and he seemed impervious to criticism, becoming infuriatingly self-opinionated and unjustifiably outspoken. When demands were made of him he withdrew into the upper offices with his textbooks; rather than studying the law of landlords and tenants or surveying technicalities, he spent hours writing fiction and poetry. Consequently, he had little hope of success when the time came for qualifying examinations:

> 'When I went up to London for the examination I despised trigonometry so successfully that I got nought for my paper in that subject ... there was the practical exam ... I was confronted with an instrument called a theodolite. I knew the purpose of the thing was to measure angles, and my test was to find the angle between the instrument and two posts. I pointed the telescope in the direction of the first post and looked through the eyepiece, but could see nothing. I therefore resolved to bluff. I swung it slowly in what I thought was the direction of the second post ... and made a guess ... The examiner looked surprised. "As a matter of fact", he told me, "you are very nearly right, but I can't give you any marks for your guess, because you omitted to take the cap from the end of the telescope." Naturally enough, I did not pass.' (14)

He was fully twenty-two years of age before entrusted with his first sale:

> 'I had at last been promoted from clerk to salesman. A ten-pound licence had been bought on my

> behalf and I stood up to sell the "Poultry and Sundries"; an assortment of boiling hens, goslings, a rabbit, puppy-dogs, pea sticks, old implements and unwanted rubbish. Trembling and sweating with terror, I mounted the rostrum, which was an upturned apple box, and offered Lot 1 – a ferret. Nobody bid ... Five shillings? Four? Three then? ... in vain I poured forth words most prodigally in praise of this straggled and wretched-looking creature, for it would have been a shame and a disgrace if I failed to sell this very first lot I had ever offered by auction ... and it was all to no avail, for I did not get a single bid. Finally, in despair I put in a bid myself and bought it for two shillings.' (15)

The long apprenticeship had not, however, been completely wasted: association with dealers, farmers and agricultural workers fuelled a lively imagination, and the hectic social life brought him into contact with two men who would have a profound influence on his future.

> 'The bar was empty and I settled myself in a chair in the corner with a pint of beer and *The Times* which happened to be lying on one of the tables. A moment later the Colonel entered ... He caught sight of me, his bright blue eyes stared angrily, he took three purposeful steps in my direction. "Sir," he said, "are you aware that you are sitting in my seat?"... He really was a terrifying old gentleman – I moved to a neighbouring chair. He grunted, ordered a whisky and sat down. "Would you care to read the paper, sir?" I said. He glared at me ... "It is for that purpose, sir," he said in a dreadful voice, "that I order it to be delivered here every morning" ' (16)

Lieutenant Colonel Arthur Steward, late of The Worcestershire Regiment, Boer War veteran, gentleman farmer and eccentric, did little work on his country estate, instead spending most of his time satisfying a passion for country sports and a thirst for whisky.

> 'You could set your watch by him. Every day he entered The Swan bar as the Abbey clock struck midday. He left for lunch at one-fifteen and returned on the dot at six in the evening. When asked if he drank a bottle a day, he joked grimly, "I spill more than that."... The Colonel never dressed in other than a Norfolk jacket, breeches, and a deer-stalker hat thatched with fishing flies. He cut a most unusual figure.
>
> 'He was whisky pickled, badger grizzled, purple nosed, pub-loving, trigger happy, bent as a hobgoblin, wheezy, arthritic, dicky-hearted, but – even at sixty-five – the best shot I have ever seen, the best stalker, the best naturalist, and incomparably the best fisherman ... and he hated rats with a passion.' (17)

John Moore was fortunate to make Steward's acquaintance. Recognising another free spirit, the old rogue tutored him in all the finer points of country lore and encouraged his first literary submissions to the sporting press. In time, 'The Colonel' became the inspiration for John Moore's best-known fictional character.

John Wilton Haines, introduced to Moore by a lawyer uncle, was from a completely different background; senior partner in a firm of Gloucester solicitors, he was also an acknowledged poet, critic and naturalist, counting many leading poets of his generation as friends. Among these was a group who lived at various times in the forest of Dean, and whom he named 'The Dymock Poets': Abercrombie, Gibson, Brooke, Drinkwater, Frost and Edward Thomas.

> 'It was in the early autumn of 1914 that I first met Edward Thomas. Robert Frost was occupying Lascelles Abercrombie's beautiful thatched cottage near

> Dymock in Gloucestershire, and Thomas had broken a bicycle journey from Wales to Hampshire to pass the night with him.' (18)

Haines and his botanist wife often accompanied those two young poets on expeditions into the forest.

> 'We spent the afternoon in wandering about the little valley of the Leadon, then full of beautiful unusual, autumn flowers, such as the primrose leaved mullein, the small teasel and the spreading bell-flower.' (19)

Thomas later attributed the inspiration for his poem 'Words' to one of their walks in the days before their friendship was interrupted by war. Frost returned to America and Thomas fell at the Battle of Arras in 1917. Haines lived on, transferring his attention to the careers of the tramp-poet, W.H. Davis, and a local genius, Ivor Gurney. Years later, he was pleased to encourage the promise he saw in early compositions by John Moore:

> 'Thank you for the poems. I will send criticism later. I will just say this. I very often get poems in which the poet has technique and nothing to say. Others where he has something to say and the technique of a clodhopper. These poems have technique and what I call content. I am very pleased with them.' (20)

Haines, who arranged the publication of several of those poems, became a valued mentor until his death in 1959.

John composed all his early literary efforts in the musty rooms above the office. He gradually increased his output with weekly newspaper reports about angling conditions on the Tewkesbury rivers for payment of a few shillings.

> 'Severn & Avon (Tewkesbury) – The floods still come up with great regularity. It is long since either

river was properly within its banks. Some nice bream were taken about mid-week in the flooded Severn. Snow water has now put a stop to fishing.' (21)

An opportunity for a complete career change came when Steward introduced him to Hugh Sheringham, angling editor of *The Field* and, as the son of a former Vicar of Tewkesbury, well known to older members of the Moore family. Sheringham accepted a number of fishing articles that appeared with such regularity under the name of John Moore that a pseudonym was suggested to avoid accusations of favouritism:

> 'He said there was a certain prejudice at HQ about the appearance of my name so many times ... I objected, but he insisted and finally suggested "Severn Bore" – I thought it unkind, but reluctantly consented.' (22)

Countless hours spent stalking trout under Steward's tutelage were not wasted and Severn Bore undertook a more ambitious project. A short book entitled *Waterside Sketches* failed to find a publisher, instead selling as a series of essays to *Fishing Gazette*, and a full length feature commissioned by Sheringham – 'Severn Salmon – Some Why's and Wherefores' – established Moore as a knowledgeable angling commentator. In 1928 John earned £38 from his pen – a sum almost equal to his annual salary. The rewards spurred him to greater effort as he needed to finance a commission in the Territorial Army, and for which he was required to buy and maintain a suitable charger and entertain in the officers' mess. It was also regarded as undesirable for an officer and gentleman to ride an ancient motorcycle, so he persuaded Ina to sell a set of dining room chairs to fund a small sports car.

The demands he and his sister made were unsustainable without a drastic change in their domestic circumstances. The house in Barton Street sold for £700 and the family moved to rented accommodation in the Gloucester Road. The house, always referred to somewhat grandly as The Gastons, was in a row of identical semi-detached council houses where Ina lived for the remainder of her life. She was, in many ways, a remarkable woman; making no changes to her life style, she continued to employ daily help and entertain friends each afternoon. Always immaculately turned out, she progressed daily through Tewkesbury, imperiously addressing everyone she recognised by surname and expecting to be deferred to as 'madam' in return. Living on interest from the sale of her house and a small trust fund, she was nevertheless held in great affection for tireless charitable work, visits to the sick and distribution of small kindnesses.

'John said the number of rejection slips he received would paper his bedroom wall.' (23)

The small semi-detached house provided little privacy and John spent more and more time in the upper offices of Moore & Sons. He completed a first novel, *The Net,* but failing to find a publisher, threw the manuscript onto the fire in temper. Sporting articles in his developing distinctive style continued to receive favourable comment:

> 'As I walked the hounds passed me, padding along so circumspectly with waving sterns and lifted head that I could have shouted for the love of them ... for their music made me mad and drunk with the sound of it and they can lead me to the river as the Pied Piper led the rats at Hamelin ... Dexter, Belman, Pitiful, Dancer, Dairymaid: I hear them in dreams, great voices belling deep down in a stream along the rocks, solitary tongues calling, threatening, yelling for blood; and then the crash of the whole pack in unison, which is like no other sound in the whole world. Next time I hear it I shall be after them as hard as I can go.' (24)

On several occasions he contemplated abandoning his articles to chance life as a full-time writer, on one occasion going as far as cycling to Kingham in Oxfordshire, in answer to an advertisement by J.W. Robertson Scott for staff on his new magazine, *The Countryman.* He was unsuccessful, although the distinguished editor promised to consider any article he cared to write. Unfortunately, his first submission created a rumpus.

'Sam' was a simple tale about a poacher caught on a July Sunday afternoon with the tails of two young cock-pheasants protruding from his pockets. The landowner accepted the explanation that they were a meal for a hungry family and permitted Sam to go on his way. Later in the day the farmer saw his freshly shot pheasants hanging in a butcher's window and the poacher emerge tucking coins into his pocket.

After publication, the editor received a reader's letter pointing out obvious discrepancies that, he said, indicated Moore knew little of pheasants or shooting: there would have been no young cock-pheasants with tails as early as July, and neither would they have been sold on the Sabbath. Robertson Scott, a stickler for detail, communicated his displeasure and, suitably chastised, John wrote in his journal:

> 'It was a mistake that landed me in a lot of trouble, but it served as a valuable lesson. I will never again give anyone cause to question my research or accuracy.' (25)

The episode fuelled Moore's dejection. Seemingly, he had no prospects of success as a businessman and little hope of finding financial security as a writer. Sporting articles earned more praise than money and poetry became a mere pastime. One poem, 'When Passion Dies', was roundly condemned in certain quarters when published in *Hutchinson's Magazine*.

> 'When Passion dies, as Passion will,
> And pulses grow more calm, until
> At last the dancing feet are still,
> And youth's hot blood grows cold –

When all the splendid madness dies
Of tears and laughter and sweet sighs,
That set such store by lips and eyes, –
These things, long since, grown old, –

'When beauty fades – the dropping rose –
And Vice and Virtue – one time foes –
Have merged into a calm repose –
Then may I die, while still
I keep some love of hair and eyes
To take across the Styx, where lies
A land that ne'er has seen such prize.
Then may I die, when Passion dies,
As Passion surely will.' (26)

> 'I always looked on the writer as likeable, with a clean, wholesome mind and with a great respect for women. I cannot imagine what has come into his life to commit such sensual garbage to print. If it is his intention to continue writing such bare filth he will lose his public.' (27)

However, those comments and Robertson Scott's rebuke did not completely destroy Moore's confidence. He continued to write articles and, beginning another novel, *Dixon's Cubs,* worked solidly for several months before seeking assistance to find a publisher.

In March 1929 Ronald Cartland, brother of the romantic novelist Barbara, and a fellow territorial officer, asked his sister's advice. She replied:

> 'Do try Raymond Savage – 25 The Haymarket, SW1. He is so good and a gentleman which makes him far easier to deal with. He is very anxious to meet you ... All the best people are going to him now, including GBS! He takes endless trouble with one.' (28)

John did so and obtained an agent who would represent his interests for the next fourteen years. Savage secured the interest of Dent and Sons, but months passed and the author had almost given up hope, when a contract unexpectedly arrived offering publication in spring 1930. In haste, he wrote a blurb for the dust jacket, before there was a change of mind:

> 'This is a story of the England that is nearly vanished; for the town creeps out and out, and one by one the old country folk die, and those that remain love the countryside so much that unwillingly they help to kill it by building houses in their favourite spots. Yet perhaps its ancient spirit lives still, and stirs and wanders beneath houses and factories – stirs in small-unnoticed weeds and in stunted bushes and in the strong, rich soil; for this is the England that is older than its oldest cities.
>
> 'The author, John Moore, is connected with a firm of estate agents – it is a pleasant existence, with county life, horses, hunting, shooting, fishing and village cricket, but at present he is obsessed with three rather incongruous ambitions: to write a play and get it staged in London; to ride a Grand National; and to hike across Europe with a tent on his back.' (29)

Dixon's Cubs, set in the first two decades of the twentieth century, is a surprisingly mature first novel to come from the pen of a twenty-two year old and surpasses any other he wrote before the Second World War. His writing always relied heavily upon personal experience and *Dixon's Cubs* established that precedent by touching contemporary issues affecting rural England. Injustice and poverty were seeds that germinated a social conscience and he used his pen to question the attitudes of the society in which he lived his early life.

John Dixon's wife died in childbirth, leaving him to raise a large family. Within a few years he met his death in a riding accident and his orphaned children came under immediate financial pressure. Dixon had lost most of his money in naïve stock market investments, thereby denying his eldest son the capital necessary for a tenancy transfer by a greedy landlord. Moore had come across such insensitive characters many times and described them well in several of his books.

Dixon's Cubs races through the dilemmas facing each member of the family as they mature and go their separate way. One girl settles to married life with a feckless husband; another becomes a nurse on the battlefields of France and the eldest boy, Ralph, a huntsman, joins the army for the duration of World War One. The poignancy of the story lies in the fate of the youngest siblings: a sensitive, aspiring writer sees service in the trenches and another, unfit for military duty and reduced to a mental wreck by malicious gossip, meets his death in the gutter. Peace brings changing fortunes for those who survive the conflict, and an unexpected windfall enables Ralph to return to farming and assist his less fortunate siblings. Throughout the novel Moore writes sympathetically about changes in rural culture, mechanisation, population displacement and poverty, before contriving an optimistic conclusion in bringing together a family affected by personal tragedy and socio-economic pressures.

Reviews for the debut novel were encouraging and it attained the best-sellers' list for one week in May. However, Moore was more pleased to receive praise in a personal letter from John Buchan, the most popular storyteller of that era. He had devoted a pleasurable weekend to reading *Dixon's Cubs,* and described it as being high quality writing of charm and freshness, with excellent passages describing the landscape and country sports. His only criticism was that the young author had included sufficient material for a trilogy between the covers of a single book. Savage sold the American rights to Houghton Mifflin of Boston, USA, but unfortunately, sales did not live up to a review it received in the *Boston Transcript*:

> 'A vivid picture of life in the English hunting shires before the war, and an equally appealing description of England after the Armistice, with the shadow of change hanging over her, and of the difficulties faced by those who went into the ranks as lads and returned as grown men, to find a land so changed from the country they had left that they could hardly believe it to be the same England they had fought for during those four weary years.' (30)

Nineteen-thirty proved a successful year: Moore wrote a number of articles for *Punch,* and sporting journals continued to take his work. Then, a commission from Hugh Sheringham gave him an introduction into an exclusive group of angling commentators – four thousand words under the title 'How to Make the Best of a Bad River', for the coarse fishing volume of the *Lonsdale Library of Sports, Games and Pastimes.* The well-written piece brought more opportunities: Eric Parker, a veteran sporting writer, suggested that Moore and Sheringham should co-edit another manual for amateur anglers, with Sheringham's brother George providing illustrations. An immediate advance of £50 made it a particularly attractive proposition to the young man, as was the agreement that he would receive royalties in equal shares with his more prestigious collaborators. He was expected, however, to earn those benefits, and the majority of the workload for *The Book of the Fly Rod* fell to him. It involved extensive travel to interview and research at a time that he was beginning another novel, and when Hugh Sheringham fell seriously ill, he had to re-assess his priorities.

He decided to abandon his articles and first told his mother. For years she had chosen to ignore the consequences of his conduct upon her brother-in-law's business and now spent a further month unsuccessfully pleading with her son to change his mind. John, however, had wasted seven years professional training, and it is most likely that the old man of seventy-six years, with patience exhausted, greeted the eventual decision with some relief.

In early 1931 John Moore turned his back on what should have proved a secure future, instead opting for the precarious existence of an author. In fairness, he had some cause for optimism: *Dixon's Cubs* was selling well, a second novel was about to be published and a third was in the planning stage. He had Parker's fishing book to finish and a ready market for sporting articles. However, the story he always told in later times about the manner of his departure was a flight of fancy. Almost wholly engaged as a writer when leaving Moores, he had for some time earned more from his pen than Uncle Tom was able to pay.

Chapter 3

A Different Course – 1931-39

'Really, I should hardly have believed that my innocent little articles would have aroused such a hornet's nest buzzing around my head.' (1)

John Moore began his new career by engineering a controversy that he believed would provide better personal publicity than anything his publisher could organise. Within forty-eight hours of freeing himself from the bonds of his uncle's employment, the *Tewkesbury Register and Gazette* published the first in a series of articles by Moore under a title 'What's Wrong With Tewkesbury'. An introductory editorial promised readers a controversial review of various matters of concern seen through the eyes of 'the brilliant young author of *Dixon's Cubs'*.

Neither editor nor writer anticipated the volatile reaction to the articles. For six weeks they occupied the front page as Moore castigated commercial self-interest and those he believed responsible for downgrading the town's environment and facilities. The Town Council took the brunt of his spleen for allowing Tewkesbury to degenerate into a venue for anglers and drunken day-trippers from the industrial Midlands. Tewkesbury, he suggested, was worthy of a better class of visitor more interested in its history and architecture. It was also his opinion that the Council would be better employed alleviating the plight of slum-dwellers rather than spend ratepayers' money clearing litter left behind by unwelcome visitors. He saw little to commend new building projects – describing the grammar school as having the architectural merit of a public urinal – and berated planning authorities for allowing uncontrolled proliferation of advertising boards at every entry to the town. He caused most offence, however, by questioning the literary merit of a book written in the previous century by Diana Craik, around which Tewkesbury had built a reputation among American tourists.

> '*John Halifax Gentleman* is a wonderful economic asset to our town ... Why the uneducated American loves it is difficult to explain. (Let me here differentiate clearly between him and the educated American, who is rarely seen on our shores ...) and it is a curious fact that next to William Shakespeare and the birthplace of Wordsworth, this strange product of modern civilisation respects John Halifax most of all his Gods and idols. Perhaps it is the connection with the word "gentleman" ... the uneducated American is a born snob ... he flocks eagerly every summer to see where his idol lived and Tewkesbury reaps a rich harvest from him ... In fact John Halifax is a monument of dullness. Its characters are as lifeless as clay, and its sentiment is so sugary, so sickly-sweet that not even the author's straightforward prose could breath life into the book.' (2)

The articles were a great embarrassment to Thomas Moore; the respected alderman and former mayor did nothing to defend his nephew when fellow councillors made it perfectly clear that they genuinely feared economic repercussions. The mayor-in-office led with a perceptive public rebuke that found approval throughout the town:

> 'The articles are the work of a naïve and immature young man, hell-bent on provoking controversy in the interests of self publicity.' (3)

> 'We have to sell our goods at competitive prices, give three months credit, pay labour ... get threatened

> with proceedings if ready cash is not available for rates ... When Mr Pickwick came to Tewkesbury he did so as a tripper, partook of food and wine and went away merry; and carried away some wine with him. A ready money client, just as a tripper of today.
>
> 'Does Moore wish to put a fence round the town to keep his so-called undesirables out? If so, will he replace the orders with a local tradesman?' (4)

Angry letters appeared in the paper for several weeks until the editor, worried about his circulation figures, demanded that his columnist justify himself. Moore only succeeded in making matters worse:

> 'I should hardly have believed that my innocent little articles would have aroused such a fuss. A few grunts and groans was the most that I expected ... Or possibly, I thought Tewkesbury would stir and turn over in its sleep and mutter, "Oh Lord! What is the fool burbling about?"
>
> 'I do believe we have to choose between the Paper Hatted Lady and the genuine visitor ... I think that the Paper Hatted Lady would be happier if she took her holidays elsewhere – choosing, if possible, somewhere where she could sit on a merry-go-round until she was sick.' (5)

The episode, intended to draw public attention to his new life as a freethinking man of letters, completely misfired, and rather than face the consequences, he fled to London. It took several years for the town to forgive him.

'It took me so long to discover that in order to practice the craft of a writer it isn't really necessary to spend most of one's time drinking gin with other writers and discussing each other's books.' (6)

A short stay in the Metropolis gave Moore pause for thought about his future. He aspired to join the fashionable young intellectuals and aesthetes attached to the original Bloomsbury Group, but they rejected the gauche country-boy. 'I cut little ice with pseuds,' he said;

> 'They are chiefly young men and women without intellects who call themselves intellectuals who hang about the inns on either side of Tottenham Court Road in the evenings. They wear peculiar clothes, have a rather dim and faded look about them, assume airs of ridiculous superiority and write poetry without punctuation and paint without perspective. They exist by borrowing from one another because they never make any money, or rely upon the charity of fathers and brothers who work for a living in a world which Bloomsbury so despises. I could tolerate them if they would show a modicum of decent humility, but they only display contempt for those who write and paint well enough to sell their productions. They are just lazy people who want to take short cuts to the production of masterpieces without any effort.
>
> '"Modernist" art and literature consists of about nine-tenths sheer bunk and one-tenth madness; with a good deal of humbug thrown in.' (7)

The few lonely weeks spent scribbling away in the garret of a low-class lodging house convinced him that there was little wrong with Tewkesbury after all. He collected together what little he had written of a new novel and returned home to finish it.

Dear Lovers, the first of Moore's novels to feature an imaginary town of Elmbury, became a simple story of the open air, clear skies and two young lovers beginning life together at a time of agricultural recession. The commentary on moral and social values revolves around contrasting consequences for working-class people subjected to the opposing forces of entrepreneurial greed and aristocratic benevolence. It was a theme to which Moore would repeatedly return throughout his career.

Sir Herbert Parity, an odious industrialist and landlord, grudgingly condescends to allow the son of a deceased tenant to prove that he is capable of continuing to manage the farm. All manner of misfortunes beset the young man, most of them undoubtedly based upon the author's personal observations of depressed farming communities. Moore came in for some criticism for exaggerating the awfulness of Parity and his equally distasteful shrew-like wife, but none had anything but praise for his graphic depictions of farming life, livestock markets, country parsons, gossiping cottagers and field sports.

Dear Lovers, published in America under the title *Raven Rough,* received good reviews and John Buchan again wrote congratulating him upon its quality. The young people, he said, were charmingly drawn with interesting supporting characters, and the Paritys conveyed unhesitating abhorrence. He was disquieted, however, by Moore's no doubt accurate and knowledgeable portrayal of English farming, which, he said, needed revival from its parlous state if England was to regain its former glory.

Moore also completed *The Book of the Fly Rod,* which appeared as a vellum-bound limited edition and contained contributions from the best practitioners in the world of fly fishing, among them an American man of letters, Ferris Greenslet, Norwegian sportsman Professor Knut Dahl and Gray Griswold, a highly experienced angler on prolific Canadian rivers. Moore, who wrote a chapter about fishing for Chub with fly, became the sole editor after Hugh Sheringham's unexpected death and was widely congratulated for bringing the work to fruition. He was, however, gracious enough to recognise his late collaborator's inspiration:

> 'He planned the book in such a way that it should treat the fly-rod in its widest possible aspect – to deal with it diversely as a magic wand which opens up a new world when flicked, as an ambassador between

> nations, as the handmaiden of philosophy, the arts and sciences, and as a friendly companion, wherever the angler wanders.' (8)

'This book is Hugh Sheringham's memorial,' proclaimed *Punch* 'and Mr Moore has made a beautiful book, contributing to it with humour and great charm.' A standard volume followed the more elaborate first edition and its popularity established the young editor among the literati of the angling world.

Dear Lovers and the fishing compendium did not generate much income, however, and the author was soon relying upon his mother's generosity in guaranteeing a small overdraft. The need to earn more became acute when he fell in love with Deidre Jones, a sweet-natured doctor's daughter who shared his enthusiasm for hunting, natural history and ornithology. Much to Ina Moore's dismay, she was also intent on an early marriage.

John pleaded with his agent, Raymond Savage, to find him commissions: he was prepared to write anything to earn a living. Healthy open-air pursuits were the vogue among the younger generation – walking, climbing, camping, cycling, swimming and sailing – and several writers exploited a ready market for travel guides. Savage secured a contract with Dents, and Moore tramped the length of Wales in the footsteps of George Henry Borrow, the nineteenth-century traveller whose books *Lavengro* and *Romany Rye* he had read in childhood. He sold his car, pulled on his walking boots and haversack, and began his journey in the North. He told Deidre that he would spend four weeks walking the length of the country and she joined him from time to time. Inevitably it took much longer than anticipated as the lovers dallied along the journey and, consequently Moore wrote *Tramping Through Wales* in great haste to meet the publisher's deadline. Intended as an informative commentary and travelogue, the book suffered from inadequate editing and attracted widespread criticism.

'My first view of Ruthin was unfavourable. I passed a number of new houses of the worst "villa residence" type, crossed the railway close to the station, where a sleepy train was snoring, and came to more ugly houses and a nasty little chapel ... Such chapels frequently shock the religious visitor ... while the irreligious marvel that people can worship their God in so joyless a manner. Its colour was slate grey, which is [also] the colour of tombstones in these parts ... the very High Altar of ugliness ... there must have been a great orgy of chapel building in Wales between 1850 and 1890; the style of that period is manifest everywhere ... Today corrugated iron has brought a new horror ... the tin tabernacle carries on the tradition more cheaply and with even more devastating effect ...'

'I would go to a restaurant and eat a large steak. Beer I must forego, since it was a Sunday and, according to the taboos and fetishes, wrong to drink beer in Wales ... Unless you have seen one, you cannot possibly imagine what a Welsh Sunday is like. It is a day of penance and black wrath, of such gloom and misery that, in Wales alone among nations, must men look forward to Monday.'

'On the bridge I saw the first folk I had met since leaving Sychant ... They were two lovers kissing ... They jumped apart like jack-in-boxes, the man to one side the bridge and the girl on the other; as if they were ashamed and thought they were doing wrong. And that made me strangely uncomfortable [as if] I had chanced upon something shamefaced and furtive ... I wondered if a brave and romantic people had been wholly crushed by the deadly influence of the chapels.' (9)

Angry letters from deacons, academics, nationalists and moralists deluged both author and publisher:

> 'It is, it seems to me, necessary to enter an emphatic protest against foolish statements that blacken the character of a nation. Books of this kind are read by people who know nothing of Wales and who may form their impressions of the country from them.
>
> 'Wales owes a great deal to these shoddy chapels. Out of them has come a renaissance of our people.' (10)

The row overshadowed some fine writing. Moore's account of the climb to the awesome summit of The Gliders from Pen-y-Pass is inspiring, and his description of exposure to violent weather while crossing Tal-y-van truly evokes the terror of isolation:

> 'Symbolic of what these mountains could do when they chose to show their power ... storms swift and sudden as death itself ... the landscape wore a cloak of drifting cloud and grey rain. And the rain was playful no longer – no longer did it caress my face with soft fingers – it lashed me ferociously ... The mist became thicker ... there was nothing in my world but a waste of slate grey water, where the white horses tossed their maned heads at walls of rock rising on each side.' (11)

It would have been preferable had he restricted himself to an empathy with landscape and nature rather than stray into sociology and politics, but only advancing years would temper his impetuosity.

Moore did receive welcome encouragement from at least one influential source: S.P.B.Mais, broadcaster and prolific travel writer, offered public encouragement in excusing his youthful exuberance and commending his intolerance of hypocrisy, humbug, ugliness, platitude and respectability. The young author had, he said, damned them all with resounding language in producing an invigorating and entertaining book. At least the fuss greatly amused one reader. Mr Lockwood, the English proprietor of the Pen-y-Gwryd Hotel in Snowdonia, wrote, 'I can identify all the characters you have written about and you have them off to a tee.'

However, the publicity adversely affected the sales of *Tramping Through Wales* and it made the author little money. He did, nevertheless, profit from several feature articles about the walks that sold to newspapers in the north-west of England, and in a series of talks broadcast on BBC Wales entitled 'A Modern Borrow' he wisely tempered his language to avoid further offence.

He had learned a salutary lesson in the pitfalls associated with his chosen profession.

'In ten years I wrote fifteen books. They are all out of print, and happily will remain so. Very few sold more than a thousand copies.' (12)

Moore wrote anything he could sell: poetry, articles, reviews and books. A few light novels and a couple of well-researched works of record shaped his style, while he made his daily bread from a series of travelogues. On a personal level, it was a time of deep frustration. He wanted the better things in life, including a stable relationship with Deidre, but reckless expenditure inevitably landed him in debt.

> 'I have not had a single week when I could sit down and write without money a worry ...all the time it has been a matter of getting one thing finished in order to get enough money to keep myself while I rush to the next – of taking rotten, ill-paid jobs for ready money – of not daring to do anything that wouldn't give a quick return ... I have never had a chance to succeed, because I could never afford to wait; never even afford to hold out for a few days for better terms ...' (13)

In 1932 Moore responded to a demand for vigorous and humorous fiction about the English countryside: it was familiar territory, and he wrote *English Comedy.* H.E.Bates, an acquaintance of Moore's and himself a successful writer, had reservations about the title. It might be taken at first sight, he wrote, as a thesis on English comic drama rather than a rollicking tale full of Wellsian characters. He was not alone in failing to appreciate Moore's play on words, the intention of which was to portray the diversity of rural England through the medium of an energetic hiker in the anecdotal style of George Henry Borrow.

The principal character, John Senlac, formerly a colourless and disenchanted clerk, inherits a small fortune and seeks relief from a dull existence by setting out one fine May morning in search of adventure. He quickly becomes involved with a series of unlikely characters: an American millionaire hiker; a professional tipster; motorcycle trial riders; a troupe of dancers; and an enigmatic Romany character reminiscent of Borrow's Petulengro. But the storylines proved too fanciful for the critics: *Woman's Journal* put it down as a trifle and J.B.Priestley reviewed it as unconvincing of reality. Only John Buchan, in a private letter, approved the author's descriptions of the eternally comic nature of everyday English life. Unsurprisingly, it did not add substantially to its author's income and he scurried away to Spain to avoid a predatory bank manager. His journey began in South Wales:

> 'Cardiff Docks on a damp, dark evening. Hundreds of ships loading, the noise an intermittent thunder all the time; with horrible imprecations filling any interval ... I walked back through Bute Street, one and a half miles long, with an awful reputation, dingy houses, awful shops (one had a notice "Tapeworm cured in 20 minutes") ... yet quiet and orderly; the people are suffering from the trade depression ...
>
> 'The Nordflinge was originally French and appears permanently filthy. My bunk is fair sized and comfortable. The saloon is roomy, but the food is

mainly eggs and bacon, and the only bad thing is the tea: stewed and with sweet skimmed milk – if I am sick it will be the tea to blame ...

'The captain is Welsh and seems very cheerful – a very old man who drinks whisky all the time, has an awful cough and spends much of his time in a sort of coma. The First Officer is deaf and also in his dotage – he may be dumb too – he hasn't spoken yet and I haven't seen his features for coal dust. I've heard he has blood pressure and is never allowed to do a shift alone. He is a very sick man, never washes, sleeps in his underclothes and never changes them ...

'Last night was a nightmare. The trimmers had a row and went on strike; the "old man" went out in his pyjamas and cursed them in Biblical language, quoting freely from Jeremiah. It seems that the whole crew are always fighting among themselves ...

'The 2nd Officer is the one bright spot – cultivated, intelligent and charming, but the wireless man is fat, dull, just married and broken hearted at being parted from his bride ...

'The ship rolls badly – it has a hush-a-bye-baby effect and I slept from 9pm to 7.30am. Boredom is a factor. There is nothing to do but look at the sea, nothing to see but the sea, if you see what I mean? No books aboard bar the Bible, a Spanish dictionary and a manual of seamanship ...

'I am reduced to talking to the ship's cat – she went on the loose last time in Lisbon and is now expecting ...

'... the deck is doing the cakewalk beneath our feet – like being on a swing that never stops. I am not, however sick, despite all the salt bacon and greasy pork ...

'Your John is such a sight as you've never seen before – covered in coal dust – just like a chimney sweep with white teeth and eyes.

'… the captain got up briefly today, but went back to bed with more whisky. I always thought the British mercantile marine was efficient; not like this. The First Officer comes on the bridge at midnight to ask if it is nearly sunrise – he never knows the time of day; doesn't know where we are or what we're doing. He exists in a daze and goes to sleep standing up. The Second Officer does all the work and worries about the responsibility. God preserve me from colliers. Even if it costs a fiver, I will catch a McAndrew boat back.

'... this is a crew of lunatics. I took a photograph of the First Officer – he is so awful – skin permanently blackened by coal dust. He says, "Some people can get their faces clean – I don't know how they do it." And in a lucid moment the captain tells me he's lost three ships already; "I lost The Hawkins there in '26," he says, pointing to a rock jutting out from the sea.' (14)

Once clear of the Bay of Biscay, the ship moved into warmer waters: in busy shipping lanes there was much to divert John's attention and his sombre mood lifted in anticipation of journey's end;

'There are hundreds of ships now on the sea; a Union Castle liner from South Africa, a big French boat, dozens of tramps and a fleet of sardine fishers – we nearly ran one down during the night. They fish without lights and the skipper was on his knees, shouting "Santa Maria, Santa Maria" but we missed him.

'It was fun signalling other ships for their names. Liners don't answer – the French always do – we finish with "Vive la France", and they reply "Rule Britannia" ...

'Lisbon is like a loom of light on the night sky and a lighthouse offshore a red pinprick ...

'The Nordflinge approached Gibraltar during the morning of Good Friday. The First Officer was on the bridge, pairing his toenails with a penknife, and the captain appeared to suffer a mild heart attack in the saloon after finishing his sixth bottle of whisky in as many days. He began to wander around the boat, asking everyone if we would reach Cardiff by nightfall. I finally lost patience and told him he was drunk, filthy, stank and was an absolute disgrace. He burst into tears and wailed, "Don't go on at me so". I turned on my heels and spoke to no-one until the ship reached landfall ...' (15)

He hurried ashore and found everything, including passport control, shut for the Holy Day, so he walked off the docks unchallenged and boarded a ferry for Algeciras. He had no planned itinerary; only a wish to explore Andalucia and during a five-hour bus journey to Malaga professed to have fallen in love for life with the region and its inhabitants:

> 'Spain, on first impressions, is wonderful, the bluest sea, redder soil and brighter greens. The roads are full of donkeys and mules with panniers each side carrying oranges and cork. People attired as if in fancy dress. There are hundreds and hundreds of goats and the fields are still ploughed by oxen. Millions of delightful children are everywhere, and for ten cents, small boys will obtain anything for you. Everyone smiles – even the beggars.' (16)

He walked over the mountains to Granada, sleeping alongside mules in barns, eating rough bread with hard cheese and drinking copious quantities of harsh red wine in tavernas. He encountered inquisitive militiamen, supped with brigands and became deeply affected by the misery of peasants. Magnificent vistas enthralled him: the Alhambra Palace against a backdrop of snow-covered mountains; the Grand Mosque of Cordoba amidst the natural beauty of endless olive groves; only when he reached Seville was the idyll shattered:

> 'There is a constant splutter of rifle fire, but the military are useless. They are incapable of suppressing anything – more die of heart failure than bullets. I am writing this in my hotel to the sound of gunfire just outside – all gone quiet now – I look out of my window, can see no corpses, so I presume the soldiers missed again.' (17)

He wrote that he would have a lot to relate on his return.

> 'I have travelled 1,500 miles by sea, walked over 200 miles, including an eight day tramp across the Sierra Nevada, and went by bus and rail for a further 250 miles. I spent £1.7.0d on food, digs, cigarettes and vast quantities of wine. The whole venture has only cost me £4, during which time I drank with a brigand, owned a mule called Jeremiah, which I bought for 100 pesetas, discovered an evil village, where no one smiled and was not marked on the map, and pursued a nymph of an English girl for 125 miles and never caught her – I received information about her progress along the way from people who thought I was chasing her. I am weary and broke, but I shall return.' (18)

A Norwegian freighter brought him back to the Port of London at the end of his only overseas trip before the outbreak of the Second World War. From that brief interlude, he set about establishing himself as an authority on Spanish politics, claiming to have been a frequent visitor when trying to secure employment as a foreign correspondent. No offers were forthcoming; instead, he wrote a number of articles and gave a series of lectures, employing a certain journalistic licence in the process:

> 'I used to go to Spain for most of my holidays ... I want to tell you what sort of country Spain is ... to compare the beautiful with the ugly, extreme wealth

with poverty, cultural sophistication with blatant savagery.

'The social structure of Spain is almost medieval. The three great pillars of that structure are church, property owners and military. Of these, the church is the biggest property owner, which is also banker, industrialist, schoolmaster and moneylender, possessing a third of the nation's wealth. There is a priest for every 900 of the population – no people on earth are so persistently harried to heaven.

'There is no sign that the people attribute the bad times to the abolition of the Monarchy and the change in methods of government. "Our trouble", say many, "is not that we have made too extreme a change; it is that the change has not been extreme enough". So a section of opinion moves towards Communism and a Soviet State.' (19)

Moore's views found favour with anti-fascist activists who invited him to speak at their rallies, a rashness not endearing him to a liberal-conservative constituency of North Gloucestershire that included many members of his own family. Quite undeterred, he continued to advance the virtues of the socialist uprising and it was not until 1937 that he sought to dispel the widely held belief that he was a participant in the Spanish conflict. In a lecture delivered at Cheltenham's Art Gallery under the title, 'The Land of Civil War', he admitted that nothing had come of expectations that he would go to Spain as a war correspondent. Some years later, when asked by the producer Wolf Mankowitz to write and narrate a television programme about his service in the International Brigade, he replied, 'I wasn't a fighter in Spain – it would be a line shoot if I were the one who did a programme about it'.

'Such an important matter as the planning out of your future work is of course something only for you to decide upon… but a little help from an onlooker is often useful …' (20)

There was no demand for a full-length book about Moore's Spanish experience, so he returned to Tewkesbury and an uncertain future. He wanted to marry Deidre, but had little hope of doing so until in a position to support her. Ina could do no more than help subsidise his expensive tastes and Daphne's obsession with hunting from her meagre annual income; yet despite those sacrifices she never openly censured either of them.

John was always full of good intentions and never in doubt that his next project would earn a fortune. He was quite unprepared to make sacrifices or abandon the good life, except that he did tire of hunting and left his sister to continue that particular family tradition. He would always remain, however, a vocal advocate for the practicalities of the sport:

> 'For some people the Devil himself is a scarlet-clad figure on horseback following his hell-hounds over our English pastures. I am no dyed in the wool foxhunter – in fact I am squeamish about the kill and the dig – but foxes must be killed – even the antis agree to that – surely it is a question of alternatives; if I were a fox I think I should prefer a two-to-one chance of escape or the immediacy of a snap of the jaws to the slow festering of the gunshot wound, or the bitter gripe of the poison. Or the long dark agony of the trap, waiting, waiting for the dreaded trapper to come in the morning ...' (21)

He turned to Jack Haines for advice about the way forward and found him in little doubt that it was time for him to develop as a naturalist and write again in the style of those who had most influenced his education: Gilbert White, Surtees, Cobbett and Borrow. Richard Church, his editor at Dents, also urged him to take stock and work steadily without the pressure of deadlines. They were both of the perceptively accurate opinion that any success would eventually come from picaresque country tales rather than esoteric prose. Unfortunately, their best advice, coming as it did from men of means, did not help with the immediacy of Moore's predicament.

Then the promise of an immediate solution, or so he thought, emerged from his own extravagancies. His contribution in the *Lonsdale Library of Sports and Pastimes* led to a friendship with publishers Douglas and Ian Service. Both were wealthy men, with a reputed annual income of £10,000, and included in their social circle others of high standing. All were dedicated to country sports and Moore was valued as a companion for his knowledge and expertise. As a result, many invitations were forthcoming and he was often away from home for days at a time, fishing the best waters in England, Wales and Scotland and shooting over magnificent sporting country. It all came at a cost, but did lead to a proposition from Douglas Service that he should collaborate with Eric Taverner, a senior sporting writer, in the production of an angling anthology. A generous advance for *The Angler's Week-End Book* came just in time to save Moore from his bank manager, but he found it difficult to buckle down to the work involved. Taverner, the architect of the publication, intended to concentrate on game fishing, leaving his more literate co-editor to research other aspects of the sport. After nine months' silence the senior partner grew impatient with Moore's failure to provide material:

> 'After perusing this list will you sit down and consider the coarse fishing part ... as I am in town more than you are, perhaps I had better do the research work. If there's anything I run across that might interest you I'll push it along. There is the question of the contract – I'd better see about that in person.' (22)

Taverner urged Moore to visit him at his home on the Isle of Wight to discuss the project and obliquely inferred irritation with the younger man's tardiness:

> 'If you take the chaise to the ancient port of Bristol ... you will sooner or later, light upon a bearded

> mariner ... Pay him his money and take passage ... you will have a fair voyage across the Atlantic ... after many days you will come to the Panama, where the hats are exported to and from Luton ... you will see clouds of mosquitoes, gnats and other noisome pests – do not mistake them for an evening hatch of duns ... Go forward to Van Diemen's land ... round towards the Indies ... reach the Great Middle Sea ... set your course towards the favoured isle ... avoid all contact with the sirens of Portsmouth and Southsea ... anchor opposite the port of Ryde ... There I will meet you and bear you to our house, and bear your charges until such time as you are refreshed or too tired to stay any longer.' (23)

There was no response. Taverner continued to organise the material and another year passed before he persuaded Moore to forward his contribution. Nevertheless, when eventually published, *The Angler's Weekend Book* was an impressive book on the ethos and practice of angling and enhanced Moore's reputation among the sport's devotees. It is debatable whether he fully deserved his share of the plaudits, but what is certain is that Taverner never worked with him again.

The delay had been a consequence of desperate need. The advance from Seeley Service went towards settling debts and John needed even more money upon which to live. Instead of fulfilling his obligations to Taverner, he had opted for immediate returns. While Taverner laboured with the anthology, Moore tried to ease his financial situation by editing a collection of his previously published magazine articles and another hastily penned novel for Dents. *King Carnival* included good stories about personalities involved in an Elmbury carnival and semi-biographical adventures of four school-friends at Malvern. They were templates for his eventual best seller, *Portrait of Elmbury*.

He chose to ignore the advice of Haines and Church by writing *The Walls are Down,* a book hailed by Dents in pre-publication publicity as his first serious work. It did not live up to expectations or excite reviewers. The story involved the complicated lives of a brother and sister disadvantaged by their stepfather's bankruptcy and early death. There is something of the author's early life in the plot and echoes of the misfortunes that befell the family after his father's death. It contained many improbable and emotional adventures counterbalanced by some fine pastoral writing.

The ever-supportive Jack Haines offered crumbs of comfort while taking an opportunity to repeat his earlier advice.

> 'It is by far your best country writing yet. You should concentrate on what you know and do best.' (24)

Moreover, a sharp reminder from another source suggested that there was no guarantee of success. *The Walls are Down* was Moore's third publication within a year and popular novelist Francis Brett Young, a fellow member of the Cheltenham Literary Society, regarded it as superficial; attributing the fault to inexperience and over-production. His advice was blunt and to the point – he had seen more than one promising writer reduced to uninspiring mechanical writing by producing two or three books every year – it was essential, he said, to learn the craft thoroughly and establish an individual style.

Moore despaired of ever breaking into the popular market, and to make matters worse, his love life began to falter. He had proposed to Deidre after a New Year's Ball without first taking Ina into his confidence. In the certain knowledge that his mother would object to any betrothal, he posted the formal announcement to *The Times* and local papers before breaking the news to her. Predictably, she placed every possible obstacle in the way, and while still largely dependant upon her for financial support, John had little hope of breaking free. After four months of open hostility, Deidre called off the engagement.

John eased his pain by taking a reflective hike through the Forest of Dean and South Wales. Raymond Savage arranged a series of talks from BBC Cardiff and the walk continued northwards through border country as far as Chester. The notes he compiled formed the basis for *The Welsh Marches* and set a standard for the successful parts of his future work. Its rustic anecdotal style followed advice given by Jack Haines and the sage was pleased:

> 'Moore has nothing in common with the conventional writer of a guide book. When he lights upon a place, he looks at it straight, with the penetrating gaze of the interpreter. If a place is mean and ugly, he says so; if it is beautiful he explodes its beauty with enthusiasm; and wherever he goes he commands the confidence of the natives and gets their spirit into his pages. He can describe the scene like an artist, or unravel a tangled knot of folklore. He is the very best of good companions.' (25)

The book captured the atmosphere of the Royal Forest of Dean: the whiff from the stacks of burning charcoal, sheep wandering over commoners' rights, sweating brows of the free-miners and forest folklore of elves, pixies, fairies and witches. It included perceptive descriptions of the Wye Valley, Black Mountains and along the banks of the Teme to Ludlow:

> 'If I had to choose one town in which to spend the rest of my life, I think my choice would be Ludlow: I do not know anywhere like it in the world.' (26)

He also enjoyed Montgomery, Welshpool and Oswestry, before picking his way along Offa's Dyke and the Glyn Valley to Lllangollen.

Haines was not Moore's only patron: John Buchan also enjoyed *Welsh Marches* which, he asserted, used the most admirable English and exhibited Moore's unique picaresque style. The generous comments encouraged several natural history articles and another series of BBC talks on Parson Herrick. Moore was at last making some progress and decided to stay with the rural theme in compiling a book featuring prominent writers who had made significant contributions to an understanding of rural England. In *Country Men* he selected those who influenced his own development: Walton, Herrick, White, Borrow and Cobbett. To please Jack Haines he included the Dymock poets – Brooke, Abercrombie, Gibson, Drinkwater and Thomas, although none fitted the description of true countrymen. It was, however, the chapter he devoted to Cobbett, written in the chronicler's same rumbustious style, that provided the most memorable piece.

Country Men was a minor triumph in that it earned its author a substantial financial return and, more importantly, convinced Jack Haines that Moore was the person to write a long-overdue biography of his friend Edward Thomas. A group of Thomas enthusiasts financed the project, little thinking that it would take four years to complete.

'If The New Forest were simply a guide-book I could more easily explain my presence ... but what better explanation than that my publishers asked me to write it.' (27)

The Edward Thomas biography did not get the attention it deserved because John Moore, in pursuit of much-needed money, next made a progress by horseback through the New Forest in the manner of Cobbett. The resulting travelogue describes a journey through the area's history, mythology and unique landscape and, in keeping with the distinctive character of its husbandry, contains several short passages revealing the author's empathy with animals. The descriptions of two hired horses, Simon and Miss Harper, are particularly memorable:

> 'My horse was called Simon. He was a tall, ugly, saturnine, philosophic sort of horse. Long experience of riding-schools, and the vicissitudes of a hireling's life, had soured and embittered him, but it had also given him his character; for it is adversity that makes philosophers. Simon had developed a hard mouth,

insensitive ribs, a lazy walk, and what appeared to be a capacity for profound and abstruse meditation. The first thing he did, when we got off the main road, was to throw forward his head and pluck a long curly frond of bracken, which he held in his mouth as a man might hold his pipe. Thus equipped, Simon began to think. He walked, trotted, or cantered obediently, but always in an abstracted and uninterested way, never for a moment losing the thread of his meditation, even when I kicked him on vigorously with my heels. All day and every day Simon thought hard and chewed the stem of his frond of bracken; and of course, I have not the faintest idea what he thought about, although later on, when I grew to know him well, I began to think that it was something to do with the Higher Mathematics. He was that sort of creature – a donnish horse. Often he stumbled and once ... he walked clean off the edge of a little bridge and fell into a stream through sheer absent-mindedness: and these lapses I put down to the Differential Calculus.

'On two occasions only did Simon lose his composure and allow the impingement of the unkind world upon the train of his sombre thoughts. The first interruption was the latch of a gate which caught in his martingale; the second was a scarlet sports car with a villainous exhaust ... [when] I daringly unfolded a flapping map upon his withers he did no more than flex back his left ear and roll his left eye to see what the cracking, flapping thing was made of.

'After that I always dropped my reins on his neck when I wanted to read my map and one morning ... I [read] two leading articles and the Parliamentary report ... although there was a high wind ... I got tired of Simon's mathematical abstractedness.'

'I left Simon in his stable and took in exchange for him a beautiful mare called Miss Harper ... she was not very easy to be leaped on; for she became restless, and spun round like a teetotum, as soon as I put my foot in the stirrup. I don't know why she was called Miss Harper, except that perhaps she was such a high-born lady, she had that air of breeding about her, that one could not possibly have called her just Sally or Jane. Miss somebody she had to be ... Even the grooms and the stable boys knew it and took no liberties.

'She had nothing of Simon's profound character. She was always on her toes, she was an inquisitive little busy body ... perpetually looking to right or left to see what the wind was doing with that paper bag or whether that dog was going to bark at her heels. And there was no unfolding the map when I was riding Miss Harper. I tried once, and only once: she arched her back and bucked ...

'It was the season of pannage, acorn dropping time; and the forest pigs, snuffling and grunting in the undergrowth, kept Miss Harper on tenterhooks all the way. It was as if [a Victorian spinster] had seen a mouse. "Oh dear, oh dear!" said Miss Harper ... and those neat trim forelegs would be placed toe-to-toe and Miss Harper would stop dead, peering anxiously into the coppice ... "Pigs!" said Miss Harper (with her flicking ears) and her feet began to dance ... and then suddenly a fat old sow would nose her way through the bracken ... followed by a horde of little naked babies. Miss Harper took one look at them and very nearly swooned. "Ooooh!" she said and up in the air she went, down and up and down again, until finally she landed with all four feet together, dancing and quivering with horror at the thought of what she had seen ... at last Miss Harper would pull herself together and sigh, "Oh dear, oh dear I was never so frightened in all my life". Then, putting all thought of the outrageous thing away from her, she would step out briskly and trot along the path.

> 'But by far the most frightening thing that Miss Harper saw ... was an entomologist with a butterfly-net ... Miss Harper nearly jumped out of her skin; and then the entomologist showed himself and apologised, and Miss Harper forgave him and sniffed at his net Simon would assuredly have eaten it ...' (28)

Anyone acquainted with horses will have met Simon and Miss Harper!

Pleasing reviews given to *The New Forest* encouraged John Moore to meander next through a hikers' paradise with which he had been familiar since childhood:

> 'The wind off the high hills blew a spatter of sleet into my face as I walked out of Cirencester along the great Fosse Way. Cotswold is my own land and the land of my fathers ...' (29)

The tale is of a somewhat bibulous jaunt between familiar haunts, more pilgrimage than guided tour across the fifty-mile limestone escarpment. *The Cotswolds* disappoints as a guide to the scenically significant upland, bleak hills and soft valleys, rushing streams and wooded slopes, medieval routes of the wool trains: all are neglected for the sake of anecdote and reminiscence. In the process Moore misses an opportunity to conduct readers around some of the most beautiful villages in England. Instead, he passes through them with hardly a word:

> 'I walked leisurely, pausing at each of the little secret villages of the Windrush valley: Taynton, the Barringtons, Windrush, Sherborne and Farmington. At each there was some remembered thing which I wanted to see again ... By Windrush that has the loveliest name of all the villages of Gloucestershire, by Sherborne with its fine parkland and its great ugly

> house, by Farmington with its pleasant village green, I came at last to Northleach ...' (30)

However, *The Cotswolds*, written for a new publisher, Chapman & Hall, generated enough enthusiasm for more of the same.

A Walk Through Surrey, unfortunately influenced by preconceived ideas about a county of which he knew little, followed much the same format:

> 'When my publishers put up to me the suggestion that I should walk through Surrey and write a book about it ... I thought, for one thing, that Surrey was simply crammed with people; that I should have to take the risk of being run over on a main road or alternatively pick my way timidly among the gardens of the big houses to which rich stockbrokers return at night to sleep. But Surrey is not so easily labelled and docketed. You couldn't select a typical landscape and call it Surrey; for there is no such thing. Surrey is at once a suburb, a slum, a wild heather-clad moor land, a spacious park, a rolling down, and London's dormitory. Old country towns, exquisite villages, the Hog's Back, pine coloured slopes, purple heather and miles of birch scrub with never a house in view.' (31)

Moore walked for six days; starting at Guildford, then along the Pilgrims Way to Tilford, through Grayshot, Hindhead, Cranleigh, Dorking to Epsom. His book was more about people he met along the way than a hiker's guide, but contained passages revealing a settled style of writing about the countryside:

> 'I walked towards Dorking through parklands where the oaks were leafy towers, where the beeches were statues carved out of light and shadow, where birch trees tossed their heads on the skyline like grazing deer.

'The fields and hedges teemed with multitudinous life. In the bean fields, my every step awoke a murmur of bees and dusty-sepia Silver Y moths got up in flights of five or six beneath my feet. Meadow-brown butterflies, those air-mice, scuttled about among the grass-heads; and, once, what I thought was a clump of the flower called borage, took to itself wings and flew away in a cloud of Common Blues. At a streamside three enormous dragon-flies, the big-bodied, hawk-like, insect-hunting Agrionids, one blue, one brown, and one yellow, were circling round like bombers ...

'I encountered bigger game too on that walk to Dorking. A leveret got up almost at my feet out of a tussock, a grey squirrel crossed the path in front of me, ran up a tree trunk, and chattered at me impudently; and a fox cub with a white tipped brush ... slunk down a hedge and into a cornfield ... I couldn't resist giving a holler to make his pretty fur-fringed ears stand up as he paused with one foot off the ground, astonished, before he leaped into the shelter of the corn.' (32)

The guide, again well received, made little money; afterwards Moore took what work he could get as a reviewer. He found it hard going:

'It is the old trouble of having no capital: if there is a delay of even a week in getting paid, I get overdrawn. What an incredible handicap this has always been. Again and again I have had to make disadvantageous contracts because I needed the cash quickly: I have agreed to write books which I shouldn't have written because of the need of a quick return: I have signed contracts for two or three books ahead, sometimes with a bad publisher because I was broke.' (33)

His mother urged him to come home, settle to a conventional job and write in his spare time.

'I am lucky to have grown up beside one of the most beautiful buildings in the world. The great Norman Abbey has loomed large over my life.' (34)

Ina Moore arranged an introduction to the recently inducted vicar of Tewkesbury; Edward Gough invited John to his study at Abbey House on the pretext of discussing an article he had written about the great church. In truth, Gough had in mind something more serious: imminent disaster threatened the ancient structure and he was in desperate need of funds to save it. The estimated cost of strengthening foundations beneath the tower and further repairs to nave, choir and chapels was £25,000. It was an almost unimaginable sum of money to raise in those days, but Gough was determined, and needed full-time assistance.

> 'He gave me a glass of sherry and pointing towards the Abbey tower said, "It's gradually crumbling away. The great fire in the sixteenth century scorched and cracked the limestone and the face is now falling off – more and more each day. I would like to think that you could be the man to help raise the £25,000 needed for repair".
>
> 'I thought myself a most unlikely candidate. The theatre, poetry, actresses, other girls, horses and trout were the chief concerns of my life, in that order. In my native town I was considered a bit of a ne'er-do-well and was known to be leftish; spending a lot of time in pubs, always generally hard up, involved in several love affairs and against most respectable institutions, being openly agnostic and a tease of clergymen in print ...
>
> 'I thought he must have made some mistake and thought he was speaking to one of my more respectable relatives.

> 'I was, however, swayed by his persuasiveness and the fact that he offered me a salaried job with offices, secretary and staff, and said I would be left largely to my own devices. Neither would I be expected to give up writing, provided that I could achieve the objectives of the appeal.
>
> ' "But" I stammered, "I think you should know that I am hopeless at managing my own affairs, let alone those of the Abbey – I don't think rich men would be prepared to part with money to me – I have no intention of altering my way of life, which does not exactly conform to your undoubted views – and furthermore I have no intention of attending church."
>
> ' "Quite, quite, quite," he repeated, "but you see I know you love the Abbey. You have written about it often and you know it even better than I do. And it fascinates me, as it does you, in the manner in which it changes colour from hour to hour in different lights. It is certainly worth saving".
>
> 'What more could I say? I was disarmed and within no time we had another glass of sherry while the vicar spoke on. It ended with him wishing me well in my efforts to raise £25,000.' (35)

Moore agreed to become Secretary of the Restoration Appeal, a position that would occupy much of his time over the next five years. It was a formidable undertaking and, apart from a few unfortunate diversions, provided a purpose and sense of direction to his life.

Work began at the end of 1934 with Moore and a young assistant taking their lead from Gough. A new organisation created by the vicar, The Friends of Tewkesbury Abbey, provided an initial thrust by persuading wealthy and influential people to commit to regular donations, but Gough had some more imaginative ideas. His principal academic interest lay with religious drama and he asked his assistant to organise fund raising performances of plays within the Abbey precincts. There was precedent for the proposal: in 1593, a severe gale blew a wooden spire from the tower, causing serious damage to the Abbey roof, and

> 'Churchwardens ventured upon themselves to effect repairs, and to raise money they did set forth three stage plays to be performed by the monks.' (36)

The vicar intended to do more than his predecessors by arranging an ambitious programme of cultural and social events for which some pessimists on the governing body predicted failure. Quite undeterred, Gough and his assistant planned for a festival to coincide with the first annual convention of The Friends in July 1935. Neville Coghill, the Shakespearean director, agreed to produce three plays – Simon Agonistes, Everyman and Noah's Flood – featuring actors from the Oxford University Drama Society. There were a number of ancillary attractions: choral, orchestral and organ recitals, readings by Poet Laureate John Masefield and various social events. The proposals incited a flood of complaint when first advertised. Members of both the religious and lay communities regarded any commercial entertainment within the consecrated area of the Abbey as an act of sacrilege. Those who knew that the staging of Everyman required a physical manifestation of God were even more incensed.

Faced with such vehement opposition, the Bishop began to have doubts, but Gough was undeterred. He harangued his detractors from the pulpit, determinedly carried on regardless of the objections and obtained the Lord Chamberlain's written authority to portray The Almighty, conditional upon the actor wearing a beard, remaining immobile and isolated from the audience! Coghill satisfied those demands by placing an unfortunate actor a hundred feet above the Great West Door, from where his amplified dreadful summons, 'Where art thou, Death, thou mighty messenger', scared the wits out of everyone. A huge gantry for temporary seating occupied the churchyard and for the first time in its history, floodlights illuminated the Abbey's exterior.

The festival opened to an invited audience. Moore had recruited an impressive group of speakers: W.S.Morrison, the local Member of Parliament and future Speaker of the House of Commons; Francis Brett Young; John Masefield; and, perhaps most surprisingly, given his outspoken agnosticism, George Bernard Shaw. Both Young and Masefield were brief, but Morrison, a tall, distinguished figure, spoke impressively:

> 'Whenever I visit this magnificent place I think of the nameless men who made it. Year by year they laboured; not in any directing capacity or conspicuous position, but strung aloft on ropes of straw or in cradles on windy and cold days – on perilous scaffolding. They had no hopes of personal immortality – they were working solely for the glory of God and their delights in good craftsmanship. Those who give to this appeal are linking themselves to the great and the good labour of the original craftsmen. One cannot go into this place without sensing the continuity of our culture. In a thousand years people will thank both the originals and the present generation for shouldering the burden caste upon them.' (37)

All those present held their breath in anticipation of Shaw's contribution. No one had any idea what he may say, the church setting and company of clergy, aristocrats and landed gentry seemingly at odds with his Fabian beliefs. In the event, with rhetoric long remembered in the town, he held the audience in the palm of his hand.

> 'I understand that I am expected to say something about the dramatic performances that you have here, because, I suppose, I am a professional playwright. For that precise reason I am not going to say anything whatever about them. Their function in this place is to get money.' (38)

He spoke poetically about the Abbey's beauty, its magnificence and unfortunate decline, and ended with typical Shavian advice about raising the huge sum necessary for its repair:

> 'What you have to do is touch all your friends who are well off. I look back over my 79 years to the days when I sometimes had only sixpence in my pocket. When I was a young man, like most who have adopted the profession of literature, I had no money, but when I had sixpence, and sometime half-a-crown, I spent it going round churches like this. Sometimes I got out of it for sixpence, but if I was nicely shown around, it did mean half-a-crown. I don't get out of it like that now! I am received by the dean or vicar, he shows me round with greatest care ... he takes me into his house and gives me tea – and then you see what position I'm in – I can't tip him half-a-crown – in the end I have to give a banker's order and pay a guinea a year to become a Friend!
>
> 'So what you have to do, those of you who are already Friends, is to pick out all your richest acquaintances – don't ask them for money – persuade them to visit this Abbey and keep on at them until they do. Then, when you know they are going, tell the vicar send him a photograph if you have one and he will do the rest!' (39)

He captured the mood of the occasion with desired effect. The five-day play festival showed only a modest profit, but by the end of that year donations stood at £10,898 and enabled immediate remedial work.

It was an impressive beginning and John Moore could have built upon it. Instead, he resigned in protest over a committee decision that he should in future concentrate on soliciting donations at the expense of a festival. The benefit of the event to commercial interests throughout the town was ignored and he therefore thought the church would be judged as only willing to take without giving something in return. He was not prepared to be associated with such a policy, but there was also another reason for distancing himself from the Appeal Office.

'There is no doubt that he fell head over heels in love with her. I know – I've seen the letters...Nothing ever came of it, but for years after he always sent her a signed copy of his books...' (40)

Moore's despairing mother, who had set such store on regular employment, was unconvinced by his excuses that he wished to return to full time writing. She knew he was besotted with another girl and registered her disapproval.

Mary Bayliss was his assistant in the Appeal Office and he had fallen in love with her almost immediately. The twenty-one year old was pretty, statuesque, intelligent, educated and organised, but laboured under a distinct disadvantage that made her totally unsuitable in Ina's eyes – her father was a manual worker. This was of no concern to the feisty Mary, who did not regard herself as inferior to anyone, and while John became increasingly lovesick, she refused to be wooed. Gifts and entreaties did not make the slightest difference and the relationship remained frustratingly platonic and businesslike. At the age of twenty-eight John found another rejection difficult to bear, so removed himself from the office and embarked upon the next phase of his capricious life.

He had no capital to tide him over and needing to earn quickly from his pen, sent off a rash of magazine articles and wrote a shallow potboiler, *Overture Beginners,* which Savage persuaded Dents to publish. He based his script upon his experience working alongside thespians during the play festival and, as with a couple of his earlier novels, it suffered from being inadequately researched and hastily written. It was another effort that he preferred to forget in later years, and the royalties it earned did not clear the small advance he received on signing the contract. Once again, he turned to his mother for funds.

No one seemed to be able to curb Moore's impetuous spending and no sooner had he abandoned the Appeal Office with its steady income of five pounds a week than he took it into his head to learn to fly. In 1930, a friend had taken him gliding over the Cotswold escarpment. He had not repeated the experience, but the seeds were sown and in the intervening years 'The Queen of the Air', Amy Johnson, who lived near Tewkesbury, became a member of his social circle and introduced him to the Gloucester Aero Club. He also formed a friendship with Michael Daunt, a larger-than-life test pilot who flew the first jet-propelled aircraft later during the Second World War. Both Daunt and Johnson were comparatively prosperous – he was very well paid and she had won £10,000 for her famous solo flight to Australia. John found their company exhilarating, and although they generously allowed him to accompany them on pleasure flights, he could never hope to match their free-spending ways.

Neither Daunt nor Johnson set the best example to a would-be flyer. Daunt's preferred form of relaxation was to perform hair-raising aerobatics and, to the consternation of the unprepared, took regular delight in testing his skills and the capabilities of an aircraft to the limits of safety. Amy Johnson also flew with some abandon:

> 'She took chances with an engine. Although enormously experienced Amy was not a polished flyer. She didn't give the impression of handling an aircraft superbly well and her landings were all a bit casual. She would just bang the aircraft down with a sort of "OK – that's that. We've arrived" attitude. On one occasion, she took me to Longmynd in a borrowed aeroplane to do some gliding. She chose a patch of rough heather to land on and we went bounding along for 30 yards or so, then one wheel got caught in a rabbit hole, and that indeed was that. We left it at the top of the Mynd to be salvaged later.' (41)

These incidents did not deter Moore, and with Ina's help he scraped together enough money for a course of instruction. He had little natural aptitude and it was fully six months before he qualified for his pilot's licence in July 1936. Thereafter, whenever he could afford to hire an aircraft, he flew with the main purpose of impressing acquaintances and girlfriends. One of his first passengers was a terrified young schoolmaster and later Poet Laureate, Cecil Day Lewis, who said a combination of turbulence, clumsy handling and an uneven landing almost put him off flying for life.

John also became romantically involved with Marie Griffin, an Aero Club member who shared his passion for flying. Together they became more and more adventurous, regularly crossing the English Channel for weekends in France, and on one flight to London touched down at RAF Northolt in circumstances resonant of that long-gone era:

> 'By all means land here. Any civilian aircraft may land at a Service Station for a fee of somewhere about half-a-crown which you pay to the duty pilot ... The thing to do is land and taxi up to the office by the green hanger at the east end – I hope in time for lunch.' (42)

The new obsession proved increasingly expensive. Lessons and qualification had cost the best part of £100 and to hire an aircraft was at least £15 each session. Eventually the bank manager accepted no more excuses and presented an ultimatum that forced John to return cap in hand to Gough for employment. Mary Bayliss had moved on and would no longer distract him. He could no longer afford the Aero Club fees so, in order to get flying time, he joined the Civil Air Guard, a corps of auxiliary volunteers attached to the Royal Air Force. Unfortunately, most available aircraft were deployed to university air squadrons so his hobby went into abeyance.

'It may be that I shall fail because I have lost that which is most precious to a writer, the margin of time. I have had to write so much and so hurriedly that I write without thinking.' (43)

The decision to abandon the idea of another festival for 1936 was a huge mistake. Without the incentive of diversionary entertainment, voluntary donations dwindled and at the end of the year fell far short of the amount required to sustain the programme of repairs to Tewkesbury Abbey. The vicar and his assistant therefore resurrected an even more ambitious event for the summer of 1937. Moore worked extremely hard and, using his theatrical contacts, obtained an introduction to the popular Shakespearean actor Donald Wolfit, who agreed to open the festival with a lecture on the revival of drama. In doing so, he guaranteed a large audience for a subsequent massed choir recital and a performance of T.S. Elliot's Murder in the Cathedral. During the ensuing week, the play alternated with the first English performance of The Virgin and the Clerk by Kingsley Porter.

The plays attracted an overall audience of 4,786 and the BBC paid a substantial fee to broadcast Wolfit's lecture and one performance of each play. Ticket sales and broadcasting rights raised £700, and a retirement collection amounted to £1,500 on the final night. The broadcast performances ensured national publicity for the cause and money continued to pour into the fund throughout the remainder of the year.

The successful week was a fitting reward for Moore's efforts. He also enjoyed the opportunity to socialise with thespians and show off the elegant and vivacious Marie. In doing so, he overstretched his account and exhausted the forbearance of his long-suffering bank manager. Henry Lodge asked to see him and sought immediate settlement of several outstanding cheques. Without means to do so, he could only turn to Ina. 'John in trouble at the bank,' recalls her diary. She marched into Lodge's office unaware of the extent of her son's indebtedness when demanding to know why her guarantee of an agreed overdraft was no longer acceptable. The situation created the first ever rift between them when Ina, after agonising for two days, informed Lodge that she would not underwrite any further debt. Severely shaken by what he unreasonably viewed as a betrayal, John fled to London. He would, he said, find work as a journalist and reviewer, complete his biography of Thomas and write another novel. Ina had at last decided it was high time she taught her thirty-year-old son a lesson, and did not try to stop him.

Within days, John wrote from the Langham Hotel with a further confirmation that he deserved his nickname – 'Johnny Head-in-Air':

> 'I've got two jobs. Giving a talk at The National and as much reviewing as I can safely do. I shall be making £12 a week, plus what I get from the books. I have the offer of a flat in No 7 St Martin's Mews and have fetched Marie. The misguided girl seems to be as fond of me as I am of her. If I get my 'certainties' up to £700 a year you mustn't be too surprised if we decide to do something about it fairly soon.' (44)

He also told his mother that Eyre and Spottiswoode had offered an advance of £75 against the compilation of another quality angling book after the style of *The Book of the Fly Rod,* using George Sheringham as illustrator once more. There was also another disclosure.

> 'I must tell you that the wench and I have got engaged. Hope it's not too severe a shock; must sound to you utterly crazy. She knows I have no money and our getting married depends entirely on what I can get in the way of a regular job ... I have never had any responsibility and it remains to be seen if I can deal with a big responsibility on my own – I won't let you down again ... Marie will write – be gentle when you reply. I hope you won't be cross or upset.' (45)

It is difficult to imagine what caused Ina greater pain: continuing fecklessness or another fiancée. A further letter did not comfort her:

> 'I have moved into the flat. We haven't decided when to get married – it all depends entirely on money. It wouldn't be very much more expensive getting married than it is at the moment. I pay £78 a year for this flat and we should pay less for an unfurnished one, then, although we are fairly economical and do things on the cheap, our meeting and going about costs us quite a bit. The trouble will be furnishing. It will have to be on hire purchase.' (46)

The engagement had already appeared in *The Times* when Lodge, obviously more concerned with balancing his ledger than client confidentiality, again summoned Ina to tell her that John was still merrily bouncing cheques and he would have to inform the police. She refused to underwrite the debt and a stern letter did nothing to produce a contrite reply: John placed all his troubles at her door without giving any assurance that he would mend his ways.

> 'I am very sorry that Mr Lodge has bothered you ... I had plenty of work and plenty of money to come, but I can't do impossibilities and make papers pay me before their appointed times, or Dents pay before they want to ... I have no money at all, so I don't quite know what to do. The whole reason is that Lodge is influenced over what has happened over your guarantee – otherwise he wouldn't worry in the least about a £16 overdraft ... I shall transfer my account and both you and Lodge will be rid of my bother. Do understand that I am desperately trying to make a living. It's nonsense to say that I think of nothing but having a good time. I am writing 12 hours a day. It does

> not help when everyone badgers me. I can and will make a success of coming to London.' (47)

He later owned to living in abject poverty for some weeks, earning a pittance for reviews and selling on the books for shillings to a street vendor. A handful of hastily written short stories, sold for half the going rate and without the knowledge of his agent, helped pay the rent; but he could not persuade any of his contacts to commission more lucrative projects.

> 'Lunch in Fleet Street with Lionel Hale. To see the editor of The Tatler – tonight dining at The Savile. I have no margin at all; if there is any delay, I get threats from the bank. I dare not settle down to write anything worthwhile or that is likely to be a success, because I have to do something quick in order to get money. Why, oh why did darling Mama suddenly take it into her head to cancel that guarantee ... I know I shall never write anything worthwhile again? And if I don't I shall be done, forgotten, finished in a year.' (48)

The final straw came at the end of October when George Sheringham died as they were about to sign a contract for the angling anthology. It was no longer a profitable proposition without a well-known illustrator, and with no one else readily available, Eyre and Spottiswoode withdrew. Moore faced complete ruination: he had no money to pay rent and could not find work as a reviewer.

> 'All the editors I contact say they are cutting down on space. I shall be roofless on Saturday. It is the most heartbreaking thing that has happened to me.' (49)

Finally admitting defeat, he left London for a pub near High Wycombe from where he wrote a melancholy letter to his mother.

> 'I shall have to admit to myself that as a journalist I am a failure – though not as a novelist I think, though I soon shall be if I don't have time to write another. Your worries about sherry parties are very unnecessary. I am not likely to have any here. Nor did I have any in London – a few people came in the evening and I had to offer them some hospitality ... and now and then, I had to take people out to lunch. Don't imagine my life is a round of what you call free dinners. I am now doubly exiled from both you and Marie, fighting the devils who seem to do me in the eye every time I get a job.' (50)

He was penniless and by the beginning of December, reduced to pleading for help. Ina made her position clear by demanding an undertaking that he would come home and secure conventional employment in return for a loan to cover the debts. She suggested that he should become a schoolmaster or apply for employment at the BBC – proposals he rejected.

> 'Yours was in its intention a very sweet, kind letter, but I warn you that if you ever write me a letter like that again I shan't answer it. If I became that last hope of the unsuccessful, a master at a prep school, it might relieve you of a certain amount of worry about me, but I don't see that it would do me any good. I am contracted to write two books by the Spring ... it is hardly likely that I should do them any better or faster if for three-quarters of the day I was wearing out my nerves in a classroom with a lot of noisy little boys ... and if I went to the BBC, that would be the end of my writing altogether ... I have got to the stage of feeling certain about failure. Nothing for it but to come home with my tail between my legs. Before this happened I was always certain of success.' (51)

He arrived back in Tewkesbury on 20 December chastened and facing an uncertain future.

'It was my luck that just when things began to get better for me, Chamberlain and the other appeasers, should fail, as every right-thinking man knew they would, and we found ourselves at war.' (52)

Lodge's threat of prosecution finally brought John to his senses. He curtailed his social activities and threw himself into work. Flatly rejecting his mother's suggestions, he returned to the festival office where Gough allowed him some free time to continue writing. He compiled a flurry of articles and poems for magazines as diverse as *Tit-Bits, The Entomologist, Woman's Pictorial* and *London Mercury,* and rushed another novel drawn from his experiences as a pilot.

Clouds of Glory is a shallow piece based upon a betrothed couple who race their aircraft around the globe from London to Australia in opposing directions. They encounter many unlikely adventures and mishaps and the book made next to nothing, its failure confirming that he, finally, should take note of advice. Jack Haines, reinforced by Eric Parker (editor of *The Lonsdale Library* and *The Field*), told him to concentrate on rural and natural history. Parker, approaching retirement, wished to leave a personal testimonial to his lifelong commitment to nature and sport, and Seeley Service agreed to publish a series under a generic title, *The English Scene.* Editions on angling, hunting, shooting, yachting and gardening were already under commission, and he asked Moore to contribute *The Countryman's England.*

Haines had previously introduced him to Gordon Bottomley, a writer and broadcaster who held the Edward Thomas archive and he arranged an appearance on a BBC natural history series with other established naturalists and broadcasters – Freddy Grisewood, A.G. Street, Ludwig Koch and Hugh Newman.

These opportunities gave Moore a period of stability and the wherewithal to pay his way, but unfortunately his return to Tewkesbury had put paid to another relationship: Marie, who favoured city life, remained in London and eventually ended the engagement. Ina, who had always regarded the girl as frivolous and very unsuitable, was not displeased.

It was also at this time that the Moore connection with the family firm ended after two hundred years – Uncle Tom died at the age of eighty-three. Thomas Weaver Moore, Freeman of the borough, three times Mayor, Abbey Warden, town councillor and magistrate had never retired, leaving his office for the last time only two days before his death.

The 1938 Tewkesbury Festival, extended to two weeks, was more ambitious than ever – two new productions by James Bridie – Tobias and the Angel and Jonah and the Whale – organ and violin recitals by world-renowned artists, and a large auction of *objet d'art*. Queen Mary, the Duchess of Gloucester and the Duke of Beaufort were among the donors, and national publicity attracted large crowds to all events. Profits doubled and fund-raising continued throughout the year; everyone predicted the completion of restoration work before the next year's event.

At the end of the festival dark clouds of war began to cast their shadow over Europe and, in common with many of his generation, the threat dominated Moore's life. His friend Ronald Cartland, now a Member of Parliament, was outspoken in his opposition to appeasement and confident that the country would be under arms within twelve months. It was not certain that there would be another Tewkesbury Festival.

Moore completed *The Life & Letters of Edward Thomas* and *Countryman's England* during the autumn. The former was a work of scholarship and record, and *Countryman's England* was a delight to everyone with an interest in the countryside:

> '[it] is a mixture of many things. There are streams in it, coverts and gardens, and hounds, and cricket on the village green; there is hay time and harvest and plough land and green fields. England means all these things to the Countryman, but it also means a good deal more. His English scene is a little world in which

> the village pub is equally as important as the village church; a world in which figures as diverse as the poacher, the blacksmith, the village policeman, and Mr Justice Shallow move and have their being ... the book is not only concerned with the pastures and woods and rivers which compose the lovely patchwork of England, it is the story of the lives of the men and women who work there.' (53)

It was unfortunate that *Countryman's England* reached the bookshops only weeks before the 1939 Declaration of War. The first edition sold quickly, but emergency restrictions prevented a reprint and by the end of the war it had been forgotten. With its prose still as fresh and relevant as when first written, the book remains a treasured read for enthusiasts.

That a similar fate befell *The Life & Letters of Edward Thomas* was Moore's greatest disappointment. Adjudged by the critics as a worthy accomplishment, the publication was further endorsed in a fulsome foreword by a former Prime Minister: David Lloyd George wrote that he was pleased that a tribute to the poet had at last been written, and described it as enthralling as any novel. Moore's account of Thomas's remarkable life captured the frustrations of a suppressed creative genius compelled by circumstances routinely to churn out essays, reviews and biographies to provide for his young family. He tackled any subject placed before him by commissioning agents, and it was not until 1913, when he met the American Robert Frost, that he thought of writing poetry. In a short space of time he composed an inspired collection of 140 poems. Tragically, he fell at the Battle of Arras in 1917 without ever being aware of the high regard in which his poetry was held by both literati and general public. Moore's biography of Thomas was published by Heinemann in the summer of 1939 and sales were such that the advance paid some years previously was soon settled; but before Moore could reap further reward a German bomb destroyed the publisher's warehouse, and it was another fifty years before the book was reissued.

The Tewkesbury Festival of 1939, long planned to celebrate the raising of a remarkable £30,000 and completion of work on the Abbey, was to prove the last. A service of thanksgiving followed performances of two new plays, The Boy David by James Barrie and Christopher Fry's The Tower. Fry, a new writer, composed the episodic pageant specifically for the festival and, as far as is known, this was its only public production. Moore later wrote of this piece:

> 'Christopher wasn't a very experienced playwright then and his play was much too long and incoherent: tremendously influenced by Eliot's Murder in the Cathedral. My copy is probably the only one in existence, because I believe it was never printed.' (54)

At the end of a successful fortnight, John Moore turned his full attention to a war now only five weeks away. Ronald Cartland had already joined his regiment and his friend was equally anxious to play a part. He wanted to fly and pestered the Air Ministry and his Member of Parliament for immediate deployment with the Civil Air Guard. W.S. Morrison sympathised with his impatience but could offer little hope of his services being required in the short term; so Moore listened to the Declaration of War on 3 September 1939 and the following morning drove to London to volunteer for service in the Fleet Air Arm.

Chapter 4

The War Years – 1939-45

'It is just like a prep school and a prep school in winter at that. Our Lieutenant Commander is rather like Charles Laughton in Mutiny on the Bounty; in fact I think he sees himself in the part' .(1)

Initially Moore did not take kindly to navy discipline. He was an independently minded thirty-two-year-old, self-opinionated, somewhat domineering, arrogant and patronising – none of which traits endeared him to hard-bitten senior hands with responsibility for licking him into shape. Accepted for aircrew in the rank of Sub Lieutenant, his first posting was to HMS *Raven* at Eastleigh in Hampshire for basic training. An officers' mess built to accommodate twenty personnel struggled with three times that number, so John found his own lodging in a nearby village. It was midnight before he secured a room and, true to form, he had insufficient cash to settle his account the following morning. There were many others in the same predicament and the paymasters had no funds:

> 'We get an allowance of £40 EVENTUALLY, to buy all the uniform, but in the meantime there are no beds – no aircraft – no staff – no parachutes – no rooms and no consideration of how we should exist.' (2)

The Commanding Officer solved the problem by giving all trainee pilots a fifteen-minute aptitude test before issuing travel warrants and sending them on indefinite leave. Three days after enlisting John was back in Tewkesbury, where he remained for six weeks. When he was recalled he continued to find training routines thoroughly irksome and nothing like his romantic expectations of service life. A hundred hours civilian flying experience counted for nothing, and Sub Lt J.C. Moore realised there was far more to military aviation than he had bargained for:

> 'We parade at 8.30am ... at 7pm we dine and go to bed. You see, apart from the flying, we have to learn about gas, ship recognition, naval history, navigation, meteorology, naval discipline, drill, mines, submarines, and God knows what else, as well as getting up to 12 words a minute in Morse, learning semaphore, firing a revolver, Lewis and Vickers machine-guns ... in addition to all that we have various flying trips in which we act as navigators to other pilots ... we are compelled to go to church and listen to most awful sermons. I flatly refuse to play rugger in the mud.' (3)

He first took to the air under the supervision of an instructor in mid-January, with age clearly against him becoming a combat flyer; instead, he was told his future lay as a ferry pilot. Bitterly disappointed and finding the training both exhausting and demanding, he spent three months under intense scrutiny before making his first solo flight.

> 'Landings never were my strong point. I think I will pass out OK, but I am a very inefficient navigator – I have always been the world's worst mathematician ...' (4)

Bitterly cold weather and continual maintenance problems with many of the obsolete aircraft deployed for training purposes impeded progress. Shortages of fuel, spares and staff contributed to delay, and deplorable living conditions deeply affected morale. Rationed food was poorly prepared and accommodation unheated; everyone slept fully clothed, and almost everyone developed influenza.

'I am in bed with flu, as are 90% of the Mess; so is my WREN servant, so is the doctor – all separately! Life is very awkward. Unfortunately, Captain Blythe is not stricken and continues to make things as unpleasant as possible for everyone.

'We have a temporary doctor – he's a Harley Street specialist. I don't know what in – but I hope longevity.' (5)

Moore found some consolation in shared experiences with a fellow trainee: the actor Ralph Richardson earned the nickname 'Pranger' after several mishaps, and their shared ineptitude forged a friendship that endured far beyond service days.

However difficult life became, Moore's ironic sense of humour did not desert him; he could always see the funny side of the irritations and petty restrictions:

'One looks forward to baths as to a party, is happy when the stove burns and almost cries with rage when it goes out. I have a new way of lighting it. I burgled a tin of polish from the batman's store with which I smear each stick and they then burn marvellously ... 'I was waiting at the station for my senior commandant. A man had an epileptic fit and I caught him as he fell. Then the train came in, so I dropped him and saluted the commandant, thinking that was far more important.' (6)

He first flew solo in an Osprey trainer on 10 April, but still had some way to go before gaining his wings. Although concentrating on improving his weaknesses in map reading, navigation and landings, he did nothing to hasten qualification by crash-landing during a test:

'The weather was very bad today. This afternoon it closed in on me and I landed in a big field somewhere near Guildford. I had to walk half a mile over plough to ask where I was ... I should be leaving next week, but I have been flying rather badly lately and I have to do another 15 hours. I don't think I am likely to get through for at least a fortnight.' (7)

He took to the air for final assessment following another twenty hours' practice, and won his wings after sixty-five hours' instruction. He had worked hard to qualify as a Navy pilot, but was disappointed not to play a more active role: it had been a romantic ideal to fly from the heaving decks of warships; instead, he joined 750 Training Squadron at RNAS *Ford* in Sussex as a staff pilot, flying trainee navigators and their instructors along corridors over southern England and the English Channel. He soon tired of the routine:

'Although I know it has got to be, I still think there is little to be said for it. It is boredom, discomfort, cold, being tired, being impatient, being on edge, being irritable; with brief moments of acute fear – but – 90% boredom.

'I don't grumble because I have a nice job – flying the Navy's aeroplanes. Getting paid £6 for doing what I used to pay £6 for doing!' (8)

At the end of his first week he experienced a second lucky escape. On 11 June Ina Moore received a telegram bearing news that her son had been involved in a flying accident; his letter soon followed:

'Yesterday I had a crash landing. Lucky enough to be unhurt. Engine failed 8 miles out to sea at eight-thousand feet. I glided down into a little field ... It caused £15.000 of damage. The CO said I had done well!'

'I finished up hanging in my straps, with four-and-a-half tons of aeroplane, its nose buried ostrich-like in the

> sand, hanging over me like the Leaning Tower of Pisa. We got away with cuts and bumps and scratches.' (9)

He remained grounded while awaiting the findings of an Admiralty Board of Inquiry:

> 'Lt J C Moore, piloting Blackburn Shark L2370 on high level bombing practice with two passengers was forced to land at Wick, West Sussex. Superficial injuries. Severe damage to nose-cone and undercarriage.' (10)

Moore later made light of the experience in a short story. The crash, he said, was witnessed by a group of labourers who ran to the scene and, mistaking the airmen for Germans, held them at bay with pitchforks and scythes until a portly and breathless constable arrived by bicycle.

Qualified pilots were in short supply and Moore was quickly cleared of blame and reinstated, but the verdict did not take account of the mental consequences of two potentially fatal incidents within a matter of weeks. With his confidence badly shaken, he was temporarily posted to ground duties.

RNAS *Ford* deployed its own small ship from Littlehampton for rescuing ditched aircrew from the English Channel and John Moore assumed temporary command, although yet again proving himself accident-prone:

> 'I had charge of a jolly little motorboat called HMS *Andora.* I never dreamed I would command a ship, however small, flying the White Ensign … Out to sea at 6am, went into a rope defence across the harbour. It took the mainmast and wireless aerial off. We changed into another boat and caste off again at 12md. Came back at 7 but couldn't get into harbour, because of tide, until 10pm. I now have a mutinous crew who missed their beer!' (11)

This mishap led to another change of duty: overall responsibility for airfield security. It was at the time of the retreat from Dunkirk and every military establishment was on high alert.

> 'The guns across the water all day and night make noises like a pack of hounds in full cry in far woods. I man a machine-gun post with four men. I have not taken my clothes off or had a bath for five days. I suffer sleep deprivation. Yesterday I heard the noise of 200 aircraft scrapping like mad – as if, up there, Satan and his fallen angels were being kicked out of heaven. I am becoming used to aircraft crashes, bombs and bullets.
>
> 'I never expected war to be easy, but I have a sort of faith that out of this defeat will come the awakening of our true spirit, our national guts that will give us victory. We haven't got down to it yet; we are a bit shocked and shaken.' (12)

The conflict in France, being only a few miles across open sea from *Ford,* concentrated his thoughts on the hazard facing everyone in England.

> 'I am writing this by "dimmit-light" as I sit in my machine-gun post waiting for the next raid. I have just heard old Chamberlain on the wireless. It makes me a little bitter to think that that wicked and foolish old man – wicked because sheer stupidity is a sin if it costs so many good men's lives – is still in government. I blame him for more than I blame the poor broken French. And what does annoy me is to remember that I was regarded as a sort of heretic whenever I said anything against him.
>
> 'This is a very dark hour. I still think we shall win. We now await the Last Blitzkrieg, the Cup Final, in which Germany and ourselves are left alone. Our very

> young airmen look forward to it as a great game; the older ones like me with a sort of contended resignation. I have had the time to acquire the experience of 32 years ... one is a bit more wily at 32 and has a better chance because of that.' (13)

He returned to flying duties in August as tension increased.

> 'How beautifully it blows! Coming back this morning I slipped down out of the clouds at 10,000 feet and saw the coastline of England ribboned with white. Coming down lower, I could see the big white spots round all the lighthouses and buoys and long, white fangs where the rocks stand up beyond the headlands. "England, girt by the triumphant sea – how triumphant you shall one day know when the story of these days is told." The Battle of Britain has been fought over that sea for the last ten days and the sea has been our ally.' (14)

Part of Luftwaffe strategy was to protect its invading squadrons from attack by destroying airfields along the south coast. *Ford* received attention on Sunday 18 August when sixty German aircraft, diving from a clear blue sky while the station slumbered after lunch, exposed a frightening lack of preparedness for a raid lasting no more than three and a half minutes. There was no early warning system and only minimal defence. Most of the staff was on weekend leave, but the raid still left twenty-six personnel dead and a hundred injured, flattening buildings, destroying aircraft and holing the runway. Air-raid sirens only began their wails as the first bombs fell, waking Moore from a siesta and sending him across the airfield to his action station. Fortunately, he escaped injury:

> 'The old Hun caught us on the hop on Sunday afternoon after dinner. It was the worst few minutes I

have spent. A big bomb exploded near me and I went head over heels, but apart from concussion and bruises, I am OK.

'After the raid we picked up casualties, fought fires and tried to save material for 4 hours. The water mains were all hit, electricity gone, armoury exploding and 4000 gallons of petrol on fire.

'Our young doctor was marvellous, driving round and over the craters in a wrecked car and shooting morphine into the dying. The WRENS were all heroines; they did first aid and made tea in the midst of all the awful shambles. No lavatories, baths, shaves or beds. We live in overalls. All my stuff is gone.

'Dive bombing is the worst thing in war. It is the ultimate horror. But we shall beat them yet: for I see that on an empty shell of a burnt out store-room someone has chalked, "Closed for Stocktaking". They can't beat spirit like that if they bomb us forever.

'Some essential services are working again. It is possible to wash. I sleep in a shattered building with a candle stuffed in a bottle for light. I don't shave or undress, and spend a great deal of time looking for a better hole when bombers come over. You cannot imagine what this place was like. Two-hundred acres of matchwood, twisted girders, wrecked vehicles and smouldering fires; everything riddled with a hundred bullet holes and a great pall of smoke hanging overall.' (15)

In September 1949 Moore wrote in an article:

'Ten years ago I set off to shoot partridge. Afterwards the party split up and I went off to the Admiralty. Within months, I found myself in the position of a partridge – being shot at. One Sunday afternoon I hid in a slit trench and watched an airfield, buildings and planes being destroyed. I was a partridge

then, crouching low in the furrows, crying, "Open and swallow me" to the unyielding earth, caught between the beaters and the guns. So Time brings its Revenges.' (16)

By the time RNAS *Ford* was reopened, 750 Squadron had moved on. Moore, posted to RNAS *Sandbanks* near Poole Harbour, learnt to fly seaplanes and graduated with an assessment as an 'average' pilot after twenty-six hours' instruction. He flew a new aircraft to 751 Squadron at Arbroath in Scotland, a base that trained navigators in safer northern skies.

'1941 is a year that I would not wish to repeat.' (17)

Moore spent Christmas Day 1940 at home, and left for London to catch the night sleeper from King's Cross on Boxing Day:

> 'I had a very interrupted journey. I arrived in London at 5.30, just in time for the beginning of its finest blitz ever. The incendiaries showered down like rain. I was giving a hand to put out about a dozen which had fallen in the street when a big bomb came howling down; it killed one of the firemen and hit me for six. I was very well cared for at a First Aid post and later saw a doctor who sent me to bed for twenty-four hours and wrote a chit for my MO. I was only stunned and bruised, with a few small cuts to my head.
>
> 'I shall never as long as I live forget London and its immortal people that night. The fires lit the whole city so that there was no blackout and you could read a paper by them in the West End. The barrage balloons looked like rosy-tummied [*sic*] fish in the sky. Saint Paul's never looked finer, nor more fantastical, in the glow reflected from great banks of orange smoke. And those incomparable people just walked about admiring the extraordinary and gorgeous spectacle of their beloved city burning, and now and then, when there was a near

> one, went down flat like good soldiers, then got up again, brushed the dust off their clothes and went on.
>
> 'At one time I saw twenty incendiary bombs burning in Piccadilly Circus and around the Café Royal and Regent Palace: they were all put out within three minutes by ordinary passers-by.' (18)

He made light of another brush with death, but on reaching Arbroath had developed severe concussion and doctors, fearing a fractured skull, admitted him to a military hospital at Kirriemuir.

> 'This is the ancestral castle of the Earl and Countess of Airlie! I have a temperature chart with no temperature and I had a peep at my history sheet – concussion, shock and multiple contusions – they are just coming out in several colours! Other patients are chiefly crashed pilots, bombed sailors or Poles with duodenal ulcers! Everyone has been more than kind.' (19)

There was no fracture and, although fit for duty within days, his stay at Arbroath was destined to be short. On 12 January 1941 he returned to Tewkesbury on embarkation leave, with no knowledge of his eventual destination. He and Daphne hunted with the Croome foxhounds on the day before he took the train to Liverpool; the following morning Ina received a telegram saying that he was leaving on the next tide. Security considerations prevented him from identifying his destination, but he expected to be away for two years.

SS *Rimutaka* sailed for New Zealand packed with returning servicemen and civilians. Personnel of 749 Squadron FAA, under the command of Lieutenant J.C.Moore, hitched a lift as far as Trinidad. The ship ran the gauntlet of U-boats across the North Atlantic to Nova Scotia through atrocious seas in sub-zero temperatures.

> 'There is a piece of the Atlantic Ocean which must be the gloomiest area on the face of the globe. A thick grey fog wraps it about: the wind snarls down from the Pole, and the snow, which it brings with it, is a sort of mad snow, swirling, whirling, demonic, and coming at you from all directions at once; it pricks your eyeballs, whichever way you turn. The seas in these parts, grey-green alternating with ink-black, heave in perpetual distress, as if they had made themselves sea-sick.
>
> 'I think this stinking weather has, on more than one occasion, saved us from a cold swim. We have had some days of very acute tension; I'd rather be bombed for a week, than this business of waiting for the thud of a torpedo. "The Captain's compliments, Sir, and will you see that your men are fully clad when they turn in. They should lay on their beds – not in them". But we have also seen an aurora and a whale and an iceberg.' (20)

It was a relief to reach the eastern seaboard of America:

> 'We are all clear, and a certain grey, old, flat iron [aircraft carrier] is ploughing along beside us, and practising with her pom-poms gives us a sense of security.' (21)

While cruising in those calmer climes Moore put the final touches to a novel he had begun after the Luftwaffe attack on RNAS *Ford*. The handwritten pages of *Wits End* travelled across the turbulent North Atlantic protected inside a rubber hot-water bottle against seawater-flooded mess-decks, and he finished it without any idea of when he would be able to send it to his agent. The moving and sensitively written love story featuring a young Battle of Britain pilot would eventually impact significantly on its author's future naval career.

RNAS *Goshawk* at Piarco was an uninviting Trinidadian location hastily constructed from a jungle clearing, consisting of a single airstrip, rough accommodation and hangers. Moore's squadron was a vanguard for fifty qualified pilots who would fly training sorties around the Caribbean in ancient aircraft carrying instructors and student navigators. The place was in a miserable state when he arrived:

> 'There are no aircraft – only one for my whole squadron; another came today, but has to be put together. Food is a problem because the navy forgot to supply refrigerators. The living quarters leak during the tropical storms and are unbearably hot in the blistering sun of the dry season.
>
> 'The airfield alternates between a shroud of dust and a slough of despair. Any aircraft which strays off the runway ends up axle deep in mud, and the damp, humid atmosphere makes engine maintenance difficult, if not sometimes impossible. The same conditions prevail to rot the wooden mainframes of older machines, and in these unreliable craft, pilots are expected to fly for eight hours a day over thick jungle and shark infested waters.
>
> 'And they are all aware that they have been given the job because they are too old, too decrepit or too inexperienced for active service. Some are middle aged; some just out of flying school; some graded below average and unfit for operations; some from front line squadrons after putting up a black of some serious nature (dangerous flying, indiscipline or drunkenness). We are a curious assortment of malcontents and feel out of the war; bitter about being pushed into a backwater and strangely homesick for air-raid sirens. Yet our job will be exacting, tiring and not without danger. No wonder many of us are jumpy and on edge at the prospect of flying sixty hours a month without the stimulus of combat.' (22)

The inactivity led to boredom and many found release in the bars and brothels of Port-of-Spain. Moore went his own way, drawn towards the company of the friendly West Indian natives. Two black airfield labourers became firm friends and he spent his off-duty time at the simple homes of Levi John and Paris, enjoying their crude rum and improvised songs. They also introduced him to the indigenous forest:

> 'The jungle fascinates me; it is like a hothouse with that damp, wet smell and queer hissing noises; a sort of whispering tenseness. The whole picture is bound up in the most extraordinary scenery; positively vulgar sunsets that would make old Turner spin in his grave; enormous butterflies; exquisite humming birds; flowers with red mouths like hungry tarts; blue, blue, fantastically blue seas.
>
> 'I adopted a sloth, but was obliged to release it because I could not provide it with enough ants. I have started to add to my collection of butterflies and bugs, and I also go duck and alligator shooting. I have bagged seventeen alligators – they are the butt of my homesickness and melancholy.' (23)

While he managed to fill his off-duty time, the frustrations of service at Piarco went on unabated. He had only two young pilots under his command and they all shared a single aircraft that was frequently out of service. Whenever it was airworthy, they took turns to fly a student and instructor, or deliver mail to neighbouring islands. Occasionally the routine was relieved by reconnaissance missions northwards to Martinique, where French warships sympathetic to the Vichy regime were blockaded. They regarded this as their only useful contribution to the real war.

The logistical problems gradually eased with the arrival of more pilots and several ancient Walrus seaplanes. Ground crews cannibalised the machines to produce a number of serviceable aircraft, and Moore's squadron at last became operational:

'At last my Shagbats were ready to fly. I tested them in the air and on the sea. I test them all myself, and then I know if any complaint about them is someone trying to work a swift one. I taught myself Night Sea flying in a priceless way. I started by doing circuits and landings at 5pm and went on until I suddenly realised it was dark. I had no lights except a searchlight on shore pointing in the direction of the wind.

'Next day I gave my chaps dual and they never knew I had only taught myself the previous night. But it was very easy: you just keep your revs at 1600 and your speed at 55 [knots] till you hear a nice sizzle and you are in the sea. Landing lights, which make you see the sea before you hit it, are inclined to put you off.' (24)

Shortly afterwards he was selected for a special assignment.

'The Commander said, "I've got a trip for you. I want you to take a Brigadier and a very important Frenchman up to St Lucia". I was delighted and had my best Walrus with engine running when they arrived. The very important Frenchman carried a small black bag. He did not look important at all. He looked as if he was going to sell dirty postcards or contraceptives. I thought he was a spy and I never saw him after St Lucia.

'His place was taken by Colonel Brown, a staff-officer who had been taking leave on the island – a veritable Falstaff in uniform, weighing in at almost nineteen stones. His luggage, a huge portmanteau, matched perfectly his vast bulk and together almost sank the rowing boat conveying him to the Walrus. My navigator, PO Liddle, crawled into the hull with the luggage; Brown squeezed himself into the crewman's seat and the Brigadier sat beside me. High hills surround the harbour, but a light breeze blowing from shore required a take-off towards them. We were grossly overloaded and my first two attempts failed.

'I decided to go right out to sea and bounce the Shagbat off the waves. I taxied for about a mile until we began to pitch in a big swell. Smaller waves went smack, smack against the hull. I turned into the wind, opened the throttle and roared towards the island. The Shagbat seemed to think she was a destroyer, ploughing through the blinding spray without showing any inclination to fly; but at last, I got her up on the stop, pulled back the wheel and started bouncing. The first two were quite small ones. The next was a leap like that of a hooked salmon. I tried to catch her as she bounced, putting the wheel forward to give her flying speed, but she plunged before the sea, into a wave with an awful smack, stuck her nose in the air and bounced again.

'At the top of this final bounce she hung about forty feet in the air. I then saw land closing on my port wing. It occurred to me that if we hit the land we should burn and if we hit the sea we should drown; borne rapidly to the bottom by the Colonel and his luggage. If by a miracle I survived, I should be court martialled.

'At this moment of crisis I glanced at The Brigadier. Unaware of any danger he was smiling benignly. He shouted in my ear, "Perhaps – though it would have been damned inconvenient – we might have managed without the smallest suitcase!"

'Then straining and shuddering, she called upon her eight-hundred horses and suddenly gripped the air. Waves and palm trees became small beneath us and we began to climb.' (25)

The near disaster was an omen. The Brigadier continued his mission, and on 26 May the party left Granada for a meeting with colonial administrators on St Vincent. At 1125hrs, RNAS *Goshawk* received a curt signal:

> 'Regret to report aircraft P5666 damaged landing Georgetown in heavy seas. Portside wing-tip float stove in. Have anchored aircraft and have police launch in attendance. Brigadier Barrington and Colonel Brown disembarked. Will report further after investigation of damage and local repair facilities.' (26)

Moore was the only casualty, having fallen heavily upon a control lever. The passengers disembarked as soon as a rescue launch arrived, leaving him and the crewman to fend for themselves. With neither spare parts nor tools, the severely damaged machine seemed stranded until assistance arrived from Trinidad. With nothing better to occupy his time, and being ostracised by the senior passengers who blamed him for their predicament, Moore recruited a local welder to begin patching the seaplane with sheet-metal salvaged from scrapped cars. Nine days after the incident there was still no news of imminent rescue and John tested the machine on three trial runs across the enclosed bay. He persuaded Barrington that it was fit to fly with a reduced payload. The colonel remained behind and after an anxious run under maximum power towards open water, the Walrus lumbered into the sky, making for the nearest navy base on St Lucia. Moore landed on a calm sea and within hours arrived in the sickbay suffering delayed shock and depression.

> 'I shall be glad when my personal war is over. I am not feeling fit and am expected to fly in to and out of places where aircraft have never been before. I am under considerable strain with a thousand little worries: fuel, spares, inadequate local labour. For the first time in my life I am dependant upon myself and have others dependant on me. My

> squadron fetches and carries and ferries and transports government despatches, GPO mail, spies, Brigadiers and staff-officers, with no proper maintenance, spares etc.' (27)

While he remained grounded, another Board of Inquiry convened, although its verdict would be inconsequential to his future deployment. Following a short period of convalescence, he was readmitted to a civilian hospital after a relapse:

> 'I am in for investigation of stomach trouble. I have another ten days here, but am getting better. The trouble started with the crash. I thought I was only bruised.' (28)

A consultant diagnosed acute traumatic cystitis and the predicted ten days stretched to four weeks before Moore could leave by ship for Trinidad. A week later he collapsed again with a bout of rheumatic fever, and doctors expressed doubts about his prospects of a full recovery:

> 'When I got back to Trinidad, I was not fit enough to fly. There was continual tropical rain and everyone got soaked four times a day. I got rheumatism. There is so much sickness. This is a devil's island and it is all the navy's fault for a lack of proper planning and ill-advised choice of sites.
>
> 'The doctors' one idea is to get me out of Trinidad. I started to get better, but did too much. The rheumatism came back and I developed a bad tummy and fever again.' (29)

His mother knew nothing of the crash or illnesses until she received a letter some weeks later. She was naturally beside herself with worry, but could not get further information from the

Admiralty; John was already at a Royal Navy auxiliary hospital at Barrow Gurney near Bristol when she next received news in a telegram:

> 'Nothing radically wrong. Just a rather tired heart. I've had two heart x-rays and an electrocardiograph, but the results aren't through.' (30)

The prognosis was not encouraging and he remained in hospital for two months until he was eventually discharged as fit only for light duties:

> 'Blast my old heart. The Admiralty haven't much use for grounded pilots. I can have an intelligence or staff job, or they lend me to the Ministry of Information or Aircraft Production.' (31)

The New Year of 1942 saw Moore posted on a secondment to RAF *Duxford* as an assistant staff officer in the Naval Air Fighting Development unit. He found it difficult to come to terms with the fact that his medical condition had put an end to flying duties.

> 'I supervise the signals about the movement of aircraft, and check on their safe arrival at their destination. I am also responsible for the fire-party and the ground and ambulance parties, and the sick bay and Lord knows what else.' (32)

While stationed at Duxford John applied for permission to publish his novel completed during the voyage to Trinidad, and in doing so, brought himself to notice as a potential propagandist in the Admiralty Press Division.

Wits End - it is written by a man on active service. The main incidents have the stamp of actuality. (33)

There had been a series of unsuccessful campaigns during the first two years of war and the Establishment was desperate to raise civilian morale. *Wits End* was a sincere and satisfying account of one pilot's involvement in a rare triumph – the Battle of Britain. The moving story of self-sacrifice and astonishing bravery during the summer of 1940 is well developed. Moore wrote with the authority of personal experience of the Blitz and technicalities of flying, and his book appeared among a short-list of publications considered suitable for general release as a full-length feature film. But paper rationing restricted the book's circulation and eventually, for political reasons, the intention of dramatising it was conveniently shelved:

> 'I do not think it would be advisable to make this the subject of a film during the war ... it would be better to hold it over till peace is with us once more. My reason is that poignancy is given to the story by the victory being won by men in often-obsolete planes and always vastly outnumbered. The reason these men were in old planes is because of authority's slothful, complacent stupidity. It makes grim reading. When the country is still at war, I feel it is useless to stress the insane blindness of facts.
>
> 'After the war is over the great epic of the Battle of Britain will acquire its true momentous importance; a film with this background would be much better timed then.' (34)

The decision was a disappointment at the particularly difficult time of Moore's readmission to hospital:

> 'My heart is still going bump. My gastritis is chiefly nervous, a manifestation of general rundowness [*sic*] and work and worry. The bumpy heart is all part of the same thing – a legacy of Trinidad and being blown up by that bomb.' (35)

There was no prospect of him flying again; when he was discharged he was posted to the Admiralty in Whitehall. Convalescent leave delayed his actual arrival and he spent a pleasant three months back in Gloucestershire writing a short history of the Fleet Air Arm. Raymond Savage negotiated a contract between publishers Chapman & Hall and the Admiralty, allowing him the proceeds in lieu of a salary for the period of his leave. During these discussions, Savage discovered that in 1938 Moore had privately negotiated an advance of £75 from the same publishers against a book describing some walks through London parks. He did not start to write it, but spent the cash without rewarding the agent and Chapman & Hall now intended to deduct the full amount from receipts on the History of the Fleet Air Arm. Savage also discovered that the author had written and sold a number of magazine articles without either his knowledge or permission from the Admiralty. Their professional relationship suffered when he threatened to inform Moore's superiors and sue for breach of contract. This unethical conduct was a direct result of Moore's extravagances. He entertained lavishly, ran both car and motorcycle, and soon his bank manager, Henry Lodge, was demanding settlement of a bank debt of £150. In a stern letter Ina pleaded with John to curtail his expenditure, but he remained sanguine about his circumstances:

> 'Chapman & Hall are printing 25,000 copies of Fleet Air Arm. I shall have £500 next year ... don't worry; you think I am spending an incredible amount, but I can assure you there is no riotous living and no mystery about my expenditure ... the motor bike isn't an extravagance as I should sell it for £4 more than I paid for it now that the basic petrol ration for cars has been cut again – and as for dangerousness, isn't it rather absurd to talk about a motor bike being dangerous to flying men in wartime! If all else fails I will sell the car for £25.
>
> 'You say I ought to have had my pay while doing the book, but that would only amount to £30 and would have

> involved me in paying back half what it earned – minimum £150 – so that would have been very foolish indeed.' (36)

He remained on leave until, passed fit for non-operational duties by a medical board, he finally joined the small Admiralty Press Division in early September. His colleagues were the writers Nicholas Monsarrat, Ludovic Kennedy and film producer Anthony Kimmins:

> 'I shall like the job – official books and all naval broadcasts are my particular line. A lot of odd jobs as well. We work from 9am – 9pm.' (37)

During the first weeks Moore wrote and produced a BBC Trafalgar Day broadcast and organised the publicity for a film première of Noel Coward's screenplay, *In Which We Serve:*

> 'It was marvellous. I have never been more moved. A distinguished audience included the King of Greece, the First Lord, the First Sea Lord, Louis Mountbatten, Noel Coward himself.' (38)

However, outward enthusiasm disguised a trough of depression caused by physical debility and shortage of money.

> 'I asked the other three Lieutenants in the department how they managed and they all said they have small private means and living costs them about £5 a week above their pay. I must get promoted or I shall pack up soon. I ought to give them a month before I ask for a relief. I feel a great sense of bitterness. After 3 years of work – 12 hours a day – for a typist's wage what have I to show? I could cope with the job if it were not for my other troubles.
>
> 'I have written out a request for promotion. The extra £12 a month would make all the difference.

Dr. John New Moore, 1840-1904

Anne Moore, nee Shirley, d.1912

Marriage of Cecil and Ina Moore, 1905

Ina Moore, 1873-1958

Above: Thomas Weaver Moore, 1855-1938

Right: Moore & Sons, High Street, Tewkesbury

Above: Tudor House, High Street, Tewkesbury

Right: John and Daphne Moore, c1912

Territorial Army detachment, c1927.
2/Lt John Moore – back row, second from right

Fleet Air Arm pilots stationed at Royal Naval Air Station, Ford in 1940. John Moore – rear row, extreme right

Right: Lucile Moore,
1916-2003

Below: Marriage of John
and Lucile Moore,
1 April 1944

Above: Lower Mill Farm, Kemerton

Left; 'The Colonel' – Lt Col Arthur Steward

Below: John Moore and Zena

John Moore in his study at Lower Mill Farm

Left: Daphne Moore at Badminton, c1980

Below: The author with Lucile in 2003

The Moore family grave in the grounds of Tewkesbury Abbey

Photograph by Graham Downie

> Exactly a year ago today, at nine in the morning, I stepped on to the gangway of the *Matarva* and came back to England. I would certainly have done many things differently if I could have it again. For one thing I would have become a civilian when I realised I could no longer fly: and I should not be in the Admiralty now. I overspend my pay by about £5 a week and it can't go on. I have often in the past come close to success and just missed it, but I think that in my service career I have come very close to a complete failure. It was all right when I was fighting, but this is a world in which we fight not the enemy, but each other – and help along not the war but ourselves. I am not good at it.
>
> 'I think my crisis will come this week – I cannot go on like this...' (39)

Moore's mood eased as the result of a chance meeting with someone eight years his senior engaged in similar work at the War Office: Major Eric Linklater, ebullient First World War veteran, author and broadcaster, listened to his troubles and gave him a shoulder to lean on. It was a turning point.

> 'John Moore had some reputation as a writer of novels and short stories celebrating his native Gloucestershire; he was scholarly and fun loving, and a fanatical enthusiast for the countryside and country life. In common with Eric he, too, loved to fish.' (40)

Linklater occupied a room at the Savile Club, a meeting place of writers, artists and intellectuals. He proposed John for membership, and by also arranging accommodation, provided the younger man with company and comfort for less money than his lonely bed sit in central London. In Moore's words,

> 'This is a most pleasant club in wartime, because it houses some nice exclusive people one wouldn't

> otherwise know at close quarters; Eric Linklater, Ivor Brown, Howard Marshall, Ralph Richardson.' (41)

More importantly, he met two other Savile Club members who would influence his future, literary agent A.D.Peters (Pete), who later represented his interests, and the novelist Compton Mackenzie, who later wrote:

> 'I met for the first time a newly elected member who everyone agreed was the most lovable new member for a long time. This was John Moore, then back from flying with the RNAS in the West Indies ... What hours of talk I had with dear friends like him.' (42)

Life at The Savile lifted Moore's depression and he quickly forgot all ideas of quitting the Navy. He spent Christmas 1942 at the club, narrating a festive programme to occupied Europe from Broadcasting House on Christmas morning before lunching with Ralph Richardson. He also made a less than enjoyable evening visit to the Savage residence: relationships were very strained between the two men, so he made his excuses and hurried back to the club.

1943 began favourably; royalty cheques from Dents and Chapman & Hall amounted to £90, and news arrived that the Publishers' Book Guild were printing a cheap edition of *Wits End* for distribution throughout the armed services. He received a guinea for every thousand copies sold. With ready cash, he was able to entertain and made a good impression. Lawrence Olivier and Vivien Leigh were dinner guests; he lunched with H.G.Wells and partied with Richardson and Gielgud. Fortunately, circumstances intervened to prevent him overspending: he was promoted to Acting Lieutenant Commander and given two special assignments that took him away from London for much of the time.

He researched and wrote an elaborate brochure – *The Navy & the Y Scheme* – aimed at recruiting commissioned officers from suitable graduates and school leavers. This necessitated extensive travel to educational establishments, all branches of the Royal

Navy and Marines, and officers' training academies. A number of colleagues from the three services and Ministry of Information were engaged in similar projects; among them Laurie Lee (*Land at War*) and H.E.Bates (*There's Freedom in the Air*). Moore was then asked to write one of a series of specialist war books for general publication. As a reward, the Ministry of Information arranged for commercial publishers to produce the books for the financial benefit of the authors. Moore's *Escort Carrier* was a factual account of the battle waged by the Royal Navy against the U-boat menace in the North Atlantic. He experienced action at first hand on board HMS *Tracker*, an aircraft carrier converted from an American freighter in the yards of Maryland and the first of many to provide air cover for merchant convoys running the gauntlet through the Atlantic Gap. Moore spent five weeks on board, witnessing the desperate cat and mouse game played between surface ships and submarines in the seven-hundred mile ocean corridor that land based aircraft could not cover:

> 'It is rather fun to be running up and down gangways and sleeping in a bunk. I haven't taken my clothes off for ten days.' (43)

He returned to write the book and found himself embroiled in a controversy that almost denied him that opportunity. Raymond Savage, again ignored by the commercial agreement, wrote embarrassing letters to *The Times* about government departments undercutting literary agents and Their Lordships of the Admiralty called John Moore to account.

> 'The letter from Savage, which I knew nothing about until it appeared, was ill-advised. It makes things devilish awkward for me as I am employed by the Admiralty. Therefore, although Savage meant well I wish him to the bottom of the sea, because *Fleet Air Arm* is going well – 8,000 subscriptions before publication, meaning at last I shall have some money.

> 'I have terminated my agreement with him and it will cause a lot of unpleasantness.' (44)

Moore, given permission to proceed with the book, asked A.D.Peters henceforth to handle his affairs.

When he returned from sea he found his room at the Savile re-let, so he slept in his office for a couple of nights before finding a room above a hairdresser's shop in Old Compton Street:

> 'Mr Mario Coda is quite nice. It is a ramshackle place, but better than nowhere – cheaper than York Chambers, though I shall have to make my own bed and clean my own shoes – the difficulty is getting called in the mornings ... One of my neighbours is a French tart who is forever leaving the front door open for her friends. We shall all have our throats cut as we lie in bed if she continues to do so, so I have placed a notice in the hallway – Prière de Fermer La Port Méfiez-vous Les Apaches. It doesn't work.' (45)

Moore completed *Escort Carrier* at the Admiralty in his spare time and in the first weeks after publication it sold 13,500 copies. Its author had no time to celebrate because he became heavily involved in preparations for the invasion of Europe.

'*When we were kicked out of the Continent in 1940, we immediately began to think about going back. Optimists who did not realise the full extent of our peril thought we might go back quite soon; better-informed people knew that we must wait for years. But there was never any doubt in anybody's mind that sooner or later we must put a great Army on the shore of Europe with all its vast stores of weapons and equipment, and maintain it there until the war was won.*' (46)

Moore, posted to Combined Operations, Supreme Allied Headquarters, was attached to a secretive section responsible for lines of supply to mainland Europe after the invasion. The movement of enormous quantities of equipment, ordnance, victuals, water and fuel, all shipped from the United Kingdom, was necessary to sustain an armed advance. Plans for delivery systems, now code-named Mulberry and Pluto, had begun immediately after the debacle of Dunkirk and construction of the various components completed at sites throughout the country. It was Moore's job to ensure that the mammoth undertaking received worldwide publicity and, at the appropriate time, the recognition it deserved.

Both projects were of a scale previously beyond the comprehension of most logisticians. Mulberry, a prefabricated harbour, was to be towed across the English Channel in reinforced concrete sections and assembled to create a facility as big as Gibraltar dockyard. Pluto, an underwater pipeline laid from England's south coast to the beachheads of France, was of a size capable of refuelling the entire invading army. These feats of engineering were crucial to the success of the largest amphibious operation ever undertaken. On D-Day itself, five divisions of fighting men carrying their own supplies landed on the beaches of Normandy, but to ensure an uninterrupted advance by the forty-five divisions that would follow within weeks, it was essential that Mulberry and Pluto should be partially operational within two days of the first assault.

Moore accompanied the construction engineers as an official 'writer' to the Admiralty. He had carefully prepared his brief, collecting every design detail and observing the construction of breakwaters, moles and piers. Watching prototypes tested in experimental tanks and the final proving trials in Weymouth Harbour, he marvelled at the scale of concrete sections resembling floating tower blocks lying at anchor in marshalling areas around the south coast.

Those months immediately before the invasion passed too slowly. Moore was not alone in his impatience to play a part in avenging the ignominious retreat of 1940 and several personal losses: Ronald Cartland, killed at Dunkirk; fallen comrades from Ford and in the West Indies; and many others he had known who would not return to their wives and families. To one particular colleague, Lt Cdr Robert Hitchens, who was awarded the Distinguished Service Order twice and the Distinguished Service Cross three times, Moore penned a salutary poem just before the European campaign began.

'The world was young when this young sailor died
And the long ships were as new as a child's toy
To him who sailed at Odysseus' side
Perhaps, from Ithaca to fabulous Troy
O world too young, too fair, too bright for leaving
When the swift storm blew up, with the rocks a-lee
And the fanged white foam and the black waves heaving
Where grey-green olives met the wine dark sea

'But from his rosy-fingered dawn of day
Into our puzzled twilight, clear as a bell
His voice speaks plain the words which you would say
If to your shipmates you could bid farewell:
"Across the steep seas where I met my end
The ship sails on; and sail thou on, my friend." ' (47)

He also wrote movingly about other wartime experiences, particularly America's contribution. Research for HMS *Tracker* gave an insight into the amount of armament it supplied, and while he was with Combined Operations his visits to the vast air bases in East Anglia brought home the bravery of the servicemen:

> 'The Forts are just going out. They look lovely and sound terrible. Few people in England appreciate the job these Forts do, except the country folk near their aerodromes who see them coming back shot to bits, and virtually swimming in blood, with about 3 dead and 3 wounded out of a crew of 10. I know a man in Suffolk who wanted to be nice to the Americans so he asked a Major who flew Forts to tea on Tuesday; but he didn't come. He was killed on Monday. So he asked two

> more to come on Saturday, but they were killed on Thursday. It's like that and as long as there are Forts going to Germany in daylight I shan't say anything against the guts of the Yanks!' (48)

At this time Moore was inspired to write his most widely read wartime piece:

> 'Today I watched the Forts going out to their great hazards
> Rising in terrible flocks from the green English meadows,
> Mounting and circling like huge birds, like buzzards,
> While the hedgerow finches fled from their flying shadows.
>
> 'They filled the still air with throbbing and thunderous clamour
> As I stood and watched by the gate into Jacob's Lane,
> And I Thought: There goes Texas, Oregon, Oklahoma,
> Michigan, Massachusetts, Vermont, Florida, Maine.
>
> 'High-hearted out of England's heart towards their grim missions
> In perilous skies rising from the green English land –
> And I watched them till their great flocks became in the distance
> A small cloud the size of a man's hand.
>
> 'I watched, and my heart lifted, while the sky throbbed and thundered,
> And slowly the quiet crept back to field and farm,
> And the Forts were as small as a gaggle of geese, as the white-fronted
> Heralds of wild winds, harbingers of storm.
>
> 'And now I wait, as one waits for a home-comer,

Till they, who are close to our hearts, come back again –
To the heart of England, Texas and Oklahoma,
Idaho, Oregon, Michigan, Vermont, Maine.' (49)

The American war correspondent Ed Morrow, who occupied a room at the Savile when he was in London, sent the poem to the *New York Times* and an editorial commended it as a meaningful contribution to Anglo-American relationships. Printed in the *Observer* and circulated by the British Council to all air bases in the United Kingdom, it was later syndicated to every Allied unit taking part in the invasion of Europe. 'I received no money,' Moore wrote to his mother, 'I willingly gave it free gratis. I couldn't make money out of [it].'

At the end of 1943 he spent a miserable Christmas in London:

> 'I am the only inhabitant of 33 Old Compton Street. There are 3 cats to feed for company. One is a French cat called Chon-Chon who made a mess in my room. Typically French – I hate her! I do wish the war would end.' (50)

The Savile was deserted; none of his friends was in residence to help lift his melancholia, but the New Year began encouragingly: 1944 was to prove the most eventful year of Moore's life. *The History of the Fleet Air Arm* sold 15,000 copies, *Wits End* appeared in Switzerland under the title *Das Gleiche Ziel* – and on a personal level, things would never be the same again.

In February, Moore took weekend leave to attend a London wedding and chaperone a friend of the bride – Lucile Douglas Stephens, a WREN of Australian birth. Normally a strong willed and determined young woman, Lucile was recovering from a broken engagement after waiting three years for the return of her dashing soldier fiancé from the battlefields of North Africa and Italy. Major Jimmy Hutton, DSO, MC, suffered the effects of continual exposure to heavy fighting and could not commit to formalising their relationship. As she waited for John Moore beneath the clock at Waterloo Station, nothing was further from her mind than that another man in uniform was about to sweep her off her feet.

The daughter of an eminent Australian surgeon, Lucile was both beautiful and intelligent. She had read English at Melbourne University, but left before graduating, instead embarking with a girlfriend on an adventure to Europe. They disembarked in southern Italy, travelled overland and arrived in London in the summer of 1938. After a year's secretarial work, she took an extended holiday in Germany with the family of Gerhard Stamer, a Kriegsmarine submariner whom she had met when his ship made a goodwill visit to Australia in 1935. They travelled through the Rhine and Moselle valleys before returning to Munich on 26 August 1939. For the first time becoming aware of some hostility, Lucile went to the British Consulate and the following day left with members of staff for Switzerland. She did not intend to accept well-intentioned advice to remain in the neutral country, but travelled across France alone and returned on the last ferry out of Calais. She was back in her bed sit to listen to the Declaration of War and volunteered for war-work on the following day.

Her first employment was peeling potatoes in a Fire Service canteen: she then drove an ambulance in the London's East End during the Blitz and, enlisting as a WREN in 1943, became chauffeur to the Commanding Officer of a Royal Naval training establishment in Hampshire. She made many friends, but was not relishing the prospect of her friend Margot's wedding so soon after the breakdown of her own relationship. She was, however, pleasantly surprised when approached by the tall, dark-haired sailor with a toothy grin – 'I'm Johnnie – you've got to be Lucile. I recognise those gorgeous eyes from Margot's description'.

After the wedding breakfast, they went on to the newlyweds' flat for dinner. Margot's obvious attempt at matchmaking proved successful when Lucile accepted John's offer of a room for the night – he later told friends that he had already decided to marry Lucile during their journey from Waterloo to The Savoy.

> 'The wedding was fun. I had flu or malaria, temp 102 and I had to be best man at the end because Harry hadn't got one. I drank all day to ease my flue; sloe gins, champagne, brandy, red wine, gins, beer and, by God, no living bug could stand up against such massed batteries and such varied attack. The hysterical atmosphere naturally affected Lula Belle [*sic*] and me so we went and thought sentimentally of Margot and Harry. What a nice way to spend a weekend.' (51)

On Sunday evening, he wrote that note to his friend Mike Daunt on Savile notepaper and Lucile returned to Hampshire early on Monday. Determined to avoid further romantic involvement, she had extracted a promise that John would not contact her again. It was a promise he could not keep; for two days he agonised and drafted letter after letter until he found the most convincing form of words:

> 'I am writing in spite of my foolish little vow that I wouldn't. In any case, I should have had to write because I have things to tell you.
>
> 'My dear, I think I had a sharper sense of loss, when I put you in a taxi on Monday morning, than I have had since goodness knows when. Then came a damnable loneliness, which has gone on ever since and I know now what I knew whenever I looked into your eyes and that funny thing happened in my tummy. I know that I am well and truly head over heels in love with you. It's gone on for three days now.' (52)

An indication of his feelings was that within the week he had told his mother about Lucile: after her tantrums during two previous engagements, he would normally only tease her about his dalliances:

> 'Her name is Charlotte and she differs from my previous ones in being a lady, a BA, not a glamour girl.' (53)

> 'A girl I know was dancing at a theatre called The Windmill (very low-they take all their clothes off) – I went to tea with 15 girls all with hardly any clothes. The tea was beastly!' (54)

> 'The actress has recovered from the flu and I am seeing her tonight after the play; you never know, you may well like this one.' (55)

This time, however, he conveyed a different message.

> 'It is not beyond the realms of possibility that I shall marry this girl. She's got green eyes and brown hair and she is good and gentle, but that is all I can tell you about her except that she is an Australian and her father a children's specialist.' (56)

Ina did not understand that her son was among thousands who, in the face of imminent danger, was desperate to form relationships in order to fulfil the primordial instinct for reproduction. True to previous form, she advised caution.

Lucile did agree to meet again and John pursued her with considerable vigour:

> 'On Sunday afternoon as I was working in the office Lucile suddenly phoned and said she had the evening free, so I rushed down to Havant ... we met at the station and caught a train to Chichester where I discovered I'd no money, nor had she. So I went to the

Police, the only thing to do, and borrowed £2 on the strength of my honest demeanour and Lucile's green eyes. Overwhelmed by the magnificence of this we bought a bottle of Algerian wine for eight shillings and drank the lot.

'Lucile had fixed for me a bed in a cottage near her camp. At 0745 next morning, I called at the camp to say goodbye. The sailor at the gate who presented arms so smartly was a bit surprised when I told him I wanted a WREN. But soon the Boson's pipe sounded over the loudspeakers and all the camp heard – "WREN Stephens to report to the Guard Room at the double" (It is probably the last time I shall exercise any authority over her). She got the morning off and we walked 10 miles through wet brown woods and fields of primrose. Then to cap it all the Captain's wife asked us to lunch – asked me, a stranger, and Lucile, a rating – it made me love my humane Service more than ever.' (57)

John was determined to marry and a barrage of letters from his mother and Lucile's hesitancy caused him to throw caution to the wind. He brought them together on what transpired as a disastrous visit to Tewkesbury. Ina bluntly told them she disapproved of any physical anticipation of marriage or unseemly haste towards wedlock. She assessed Lucile as a nice, sensible girl, not a 'piece of fluff' as so many of the others had been – but that was as far as she would go. John did not intend to allow his mother to wreck another relationship and curtailed the visit. Within days, he sent unwelcome news from the safe distance of London.

'She has made up her silly little mind at last. Now says she'd like to get married anytime, but how to do it in the midst of this turmoil.' (58)

Another close call spurred him into finding the time: a bomb exploded in Old Compton Street while he was at work, destroying all his possessions and rendering him homeless. It was his fifth potentially fatal encounter of the war and he thought his luck could not last much longer.

He placed an engagement notice in *The Times* and obtained a special licence to marry at Caxton Hall on 1 April 1944. The couple planned a quiet affair, and John pointedly told Ina that it would be most unwise for her to travel to bomb-ravaged London.

Six weeks after first meeting, John and Lucile were married in their everyday uniforms, at what John described as a sordid, dismal and hurried ceremony. He hosted a lunch for six guests at the Gargoyle Club in Soho and entertained a few more friends at the Savile in the evening. There was no time for a honeymoon: John immediately returned to his office and Lucile to her duties at Eastleigh.

The following weekend, after an exhausting voyage of inspection of Mulberry holding-stations along southern and western coastlines, John found a message awaiting him. His mother was distressed:

> 'Your old friends heard about your wedding. Although, alas, I was not at it, I took the greatest interest. They might have rung me up and told me about it.' (59)

He did his best to make amends:

> 'I got back late last night, very dirty, tired and unshaven ... I'm here for a few days. I'll try to tell you something about the wedding.' (60)

Ina could do nothing other than accept a *fait accompli* and, to her credit, offered her new daughter-in-law support during difficult days that lay ahead. There were, however, no further visits to Tewkesbury: the invasion loomed and everyone under orders stayed within designated areas for security reasons.

RN Party 1500, c/o GPO London. This is my address. Can't say anymore. I want you to know, dearest mother, that I am very content, very easy in mind about everything, and prepared for whatever may come along. (61)

Lt Cdr Moore boarded HMS *Despatch* at Portsmouth at the end of May. Final preparations were under way, but he was determined to make the most of any free time in the company of Lucile before the armada sailed. His journal gives some insight into the intense atmosphere of those last few days:

> 'On Whit Sunday I picnicked with Lucile in meadows behind Havant. We picked wild flowers and walked the salt flats amid the sea smells. There is a pervading sense of this impending THING and Lucile cried at the station as we parted.
>
> 'On Monday we drew kit. The weather is brilliant; is this a hostage to fortune?
>
> Tuesday I went ashore. Had lunch with Ludo [Kennedy] and then a picnic with Lucile, followed by a long walk.
>
> 'Wednesday – out to sea – firing practice. Portsmouth in the evening. Strangely quiet, now that the soldiers are embarked, and there is no leave in many of the ships. More beer in the pubs! The civilians must know, or guess. But they are wonderfully reticent, as everyone has been these past two months. Never has the public kept its mouth shut so well.
>
> 'Thursday – Boat to Portsmouth early to borrow aircraft to photograph concentration of our stuff off Selsey Bill. These Phoenixes and Whales, moored out to sea, look like a vast factory town, chimneys and all. An extraordinary sight. A long walk with Lucile over Portsdown Hill – finding flowers, orchids, ragged robin, Brookline [*sic*]. Tea in a roadside cafe and dinner at Queens. Back to ship in PO's boat at 10 o'clock. Huge

activity, but so quiet, almost invisible. The grey ships are still at anchor.

'Friday – The Press are called up today – not much longer now. Drew assault rations. Photographs of embarkation on the Hards. Forecast says wind will freshen, damn. Taking on various and mysterious kinds of stores. Winston, Smuts and Admiral Ramsay were there on the Hards.

'Saturday – Ashore again. Final picnic with Lucile. Phones cut off in dockyard. A WREN friend of Lucile's says, "we've all got to come in tomorrow – 200 of us – we're usually in Surrey – I'm getting excited." Very bad security! A great sense of urgency back on board. A sure sign of moving – the navigator's carrying about his charts!

'Sunday – By my guess we should have sailed today. But low cloud and strong winds. Many rumours and serious faces. Embarked troops are getting stale. What about the innumerable problems of security – since so many people have already been briefed? These are more than just disquieting thoughts. Walked up and down the quarterdeck thinking that perhaps the fate of a generation may depend upon a strong depression. A heavy sense of frustration. By present plans my party moves to *Aristocrat* tomorrow.

'Monday – Today the deep depression has passed, but there are secondaries [*sic*] in its wake. It is still windy, white tops to the waves, and a blue-and-grey patch sky which is rather greasy looking. Now one is conscious of the huge responsibility of Eisenhower and his staff who have to give the word "Go" in weather that leaves a very narrow margin between success and disaster. Meanwhile the work of the ship goes on. In the good tradition of the Navy, we are actually painting ship before battle. It is good to go into battle looking smart.

Arrival of new officers – RNVR Captain, a Brigadier and high ranking Engineers. The Padre is not coming with us – Somebody says, "Pity Padre, you'd get more funerals with us."

'During the afternoon, there is a gradual – very gradual – improvement in the weather. At 4.30, the wind begins to drop and soon we see signs that in spite of still threatening skies, Operation Overlord is beginning. In the evening, we watch the greatest Armada the world has ever seen going out to battle. One could not help thinking that now we have committed at last, now we have hazarded all – an awe-inspiring thought.

'At 2100 hours, the Captain announces the invasion to all hands. He explains Mulberry and tells them they are a hand picked lot for a hand picked job. Officers briefed afterwards in the wardroom. Brigadier Walter warns that once The Hun knows what we are up to he will become very interested in us indeed.

'Tuesday – D-Day – The invasion is announced on the 8 o'clock news. Idiotic publicity. The weather is not good, but the army is ashore. Transferred to *Aristocrat* and we are on our way. So much shipping – a maritime Piccadilly Circus – hard to believe we sent 2,000 ships last night. We meet returning ships and through the binoculars see bareheaded men. They are burying chaps at sea – saw one go over the side. The weather deteriorates. Feel seasick and only get a little fitful sleep on a sofa in the wardroom. Up at 5 to a greasy pewter coloured dawn. The flotsam of war is floating by.' (62)

The huge prefabricated sections of Mulberry proceeded from their assembly-points to cross the English Channel, towed by two hundred tugs at a speed of four knots. The first elements arrived at the small port of Arromanches-les-Baines in Normandy while battle still raged for domination of the beachheads. Work on the floating harbour, comprising one and a half million tons of reinforced concrete, began immediately. General Eisenhower intended to move 850,000 fighting men, their supplies and 150,000 vehicles into France by the end of June.

HMS *Aristocrat*, accompanied by the sixty obsolete ships that created a breakwater when scuttled, arrived off Arromanches during the evening of D-Day. The demolition teams started work under the protection of salvos from an offshore battle fleet and covering squadrons of aircraft. Their deafening din and additional noise from heavy inshore fighting convinced John Moore that he was unlikely to survive the night. Sinking the block-ships continued in improved weather throughout D-Day-plus-one as more sections of Mulberry eased into position through lanes of landing craft and assault ships taking troops ashore. The concrete lockers queued over a distance of five miles before manoeuvring to form the wall and piers of a harbour that would bear twelve miles of tracks extending towards new road routes blasted through the buildings of Arromanches.

> 'We put the whole 7th Armoured Div ashore today. The Sappers flattened more houses and blew up the sea wall. Not one windowpane remains intact throughout the whole village. If these people hate us in a week's time I shan't blame them, they will have reason. I went ashore and spoke to them; there was no hostility – the war is "beaucoup malheureuse" they said – and they are bloody right!' (63)

Then, thirteen days after D-Day, another capricious weather system threatened disastrous delay:

> 'Towards evening the barometer began to fall and the wind increased throughout the night.
>
> 'We didn't get our usual dawn visits by the snooping Fockers nor hear the Spits and other

marauders streaming over, for the cloud was down to 500 feet, the balloons were faint grey shadows overhead, and the wind was whipping up white horses on the pewter-coloured sea.

'It blew all morning and all afternoon, but the sky seemed brighter in the north, and we told ourselves: "It can't last. A gale can't possibly last long in June."

'By now it was indeed a gale. We reckoned it was blowing Force 8, and stronger in the gusts. It came from the north, with a touch of east in it, and that was the worst direction, for it piled up the seas on our north-facing beaches and created the very condition which is the mariner's ancient peril and ancient dread; a lee shore, on which even great ships can meet their doom and small ones are smashed to matchwood.

'Most of our ships were small ones, and they stood off-shore, head to wind, riding it out. There must have been hundreds of ships at peril there. At dusk, I looked seaward and saw the white surf creaming their bows even though they lay at their anchors. With the darkness, the wind came stronger. It was a very dark night, but inland to the south of us the sky was lit by the summer-lightning flicker of the guns. We could not hear the battle; the wind was too strong. But the flashes reminded us that we had a great army ashore, which was eating up its supplies. Every tank, lorry, gun, rifle and man had to be fed. Each time a convoy moved or a tank-patrol went out or a Battery fired the dumps behind the lines were that much smaller. And we could not replenish the dumps while the wind blew. The full flood of our supplies had dried up to a trickle.

'A thousand difficulties piled upon us. Tows still on the way across are lost, the concrete bombardons are breaking up, the piers writhe like snakes and moan and groan. Its balls to say that God is on our side, it is hell The difficulty of dealing with the sea – you are

> playing with the most powerful force in the world. And we begin to get a terrible amount of flotsam and jetsam on our beaches: upturned boats, lorries, a twenty-five pounder gun, motor cycles and corpses. And the attack was suspended.
>
> 'On the third day it still blew, perhaps not as fiercely, but the situation ashore was more critical. It was the worst and longest day. It was as if there was no past without the gale, it had blown forever, and no still future, it would never cease. We lost a lot of little ships – it is terrible to see the craft broached-to and to see the surf savage it, crush it like a dog with a bone.
>
> 'But in the evening the clouds lifted a bit and the shriek of the wind in the shrouds was less of a shriek than a long drawn sigh. We heard a murmur in the sky that grew to a great roar and watched Dakotas going over with supplies and return with the wounded. They were a more welcome sight to us than ever the first swallow has been; for beyond them, in the sky to the northward, there was a long ragged rent, a patch big enough to make a Dutchman a pair of trousers, a harbinger of better weather to come.
>
> 'And then suddenly – it was as if we saw it for the first time – the sun shone.' [(64)]

Calmer seas exposed extensive damage, but recovery teams worked to such good effect that over the next three months two million men, half a million vehicles and four million tons of supplies passed through the harbour.

The staff who ran and maintained Mulberry settled in for a long haul. A fleet of accommodation ships docked on the leeward side became their homes; local supplies supplemented rations and motor launches delivered mail, newspapers, fresh water and bread, as life assumed a loose normality amid round-the-clock activity. Once the fighting moved inland, John Moore explored the countryside, milking cows neglected by fleeing farmers and avoiding mines in a search for wild flowers. In quieter moments, he reflected on the scale of the invasion:

> 'One evening I stood on the sea wall at Arromanches and looked backwards towards England. The ships lay so close together that they were like stepping-stones across the channel; you felt you could walk all the way to Portsmouth jumping from one to another. Back on the beach, the young charioteers of armoured divisions rode ashore. Somehow, my sense awakened of the splendour of what we had done: the awful splendour of D-Day, and I thought that whatever glorious things had happened before, or would happen henceforth, could not match or dim it. It was a day to put beside Thermoplae and Trafalgar.' (65)

Moore's direct involvement in the invasion of Europe ended in September when he returned to the Admiralty to edit a film and write the official report about Mulberry.

> 'The whole of the Naval Staff wanted to see me and hear about our job, but I have never felt so consistently tired as I do now. It's a reaction from four months of planning and keeping secrets, and then being keyed up to be killed, and then not being killed.' (66)

He saw little of Lucile and, therefore, did not detect the signs of her deteriorating health. She became depressed and, dreading another winter in communal barracks, applied to terminate her service. She then developed an unidentified serious illness while awaiting the decision and was admitted to a Royal Navy hospital. Perplexed doctors transferred her to the Westminster Hospital in London.

> I have just had a very bad shock. Lucile was X-rayed and I saw her doctor today. They thought she

had TB and would need a minimum of nine months treatment.

'Now they have taken more X-Rays and there is a sort of granular condition in the lungs, but the doctors don't agree on the cause. The TB tests are now negative and they say that when she's seen the specialist she can be released, but I don't know where she will go.' (67)

Hospitals throughout the United Kingdom were struggling to cope with military casualties and came under enormous pressure to free all possible bed-space. John could not consider caring for Lucile in his London bedsit and, not for the first time, turned to his mother. Lucile was discharged from the WRNS on medical grounds, taken to Tewkesbury by naval medical staff and transferred to the care of a local doctor who proved more percipient and resourceful than the London consultants.

Dr Hopper-Shepherd was a family friend and sympathetic to those in uniform: he grieved for one son killed in action, while another had received the Military Cross twice for bravery. He was from the old school of medicine, possessed of a gentle, confident bedside manner and willingness to listen. Initially Lucile's condition baffled him, but he persuaded John to contact her parents by cable for information about any childhood diseases that may have a bearing on her current illness. The response was immediate. Dr Stephens, who until that time had known nothing of his daughter's condition, revealed that she was treated in infancy for a lung condition that he thought could now have recurred in the more serious form of Sarciodosis. Tests confirmed his diagnosis; Hopper-Shepherd prescribed appropriate treatment and predicted a full recovery.

Lucile remained quite ill for some time and Moore, on compassionate unpaid leave, stayed with her. Ina took great care of her daughter-in-law and John accepted Lucile's suggestion as to how he might usefully occupy his time. In doing so, he changed the course of their lives.

'We were pretty broke. We had nowhere to live and no furniture if we found somewhere. I told John he had better get writing.' (68)

For some years, he had toyed with the notion of writing an anecdotal book about his early years in Tewkesbury and found A.D.Peters receptive to the idea. Peters negotiated a contract and advance of £300 with Collins, and Moore completed *Portrait of Elmbury* in six weeks. He returned to the Admiralty in January 1945 with a wife well on the road to recovery and another book in the pipeline.

Portrait of Elmbury reached bookshops in October, and Moore looked forward to an early return to civilian life now that war was over.

Chapter 5

Post-War Success – 1945-51

'I have written a book which gives me much pleasure. It is a kind of full-length portrait of a small country town – this small town – between the wars. The sort of life that will never come back.' (1)

Moore spent little time at the Admiralty during that last year, being more usually at home writing and caring for Lucile. Colleagues in the Press Department covered for him during prolonged unauthorised absences – Nicholas Monsarrat wrote that there was little going on and advised him to keep his head down!

Portrait of Elmbury was an immediate success, its appeal lying in a fund of nostalgic stories about an era to which a population, wearied by war, yearned to return. In fact, it contained so many identifiable people and occurrences that Moore felt obliged to begin with a disclaimer:

> 'This account of the fortunes of people is built upon a framework of truth, but I haven't hesitated to alter names, to play tricks with time and geography, and where necessary to import one or two original and purely imaginary wrongdoers.' (2)

It became a consuming pastime for Tewkesbury people to put names to the book's characters and Ina Moore lived in a state of embarrassment and fear of litigation, until a friend assured her that John had a recipe for successfully clouding fact with fiction:

> 'Mike Shepherd told her I was an acute observer of people, absorbing the gait and style of those I met,

> their way of dressing and their way of speech; their individual likes and dislikes, as well as their special interests. So it is natural that I should model my characters not on one, but create an amalgam of many. Sometimes I was tempted to exaggeration; producing larger than life, fantastical characters, more entertaining than any living person, who were intended to place the book on a plane above the humdrum and dullness of rural life.' (3)

One example of this is his endearing portrayal of 'The Colonel', owed in large part to Arthur Steward, the elderly eccentric sporting companion of his youth. Had he lived long enough to read the book, Steward, a gentleman of Victorian manners, may well have objected to Moore's magnificent depiction of a whisky-pickled maverick with complete disregard for the sensitivities of polite society. Moreover, there would no doubt have been fearsome reprisals from 'Black Sal', a disreputable harridan based upon the real-life 'Black Shuck' of the alleys who was well acquainted with Tewkesbury magistrates:

> 'She always wore black from head to toe. She was mad, she was frequently drunk and she never washed. When the frenzy came upon her, or when she was full of gin, she would range about the town chanting meaningless obscenities; at other times she practiced a kind of coarse and friendly banter, a running commentary upon life and affairs, addressed to all and sundry, but particularly to the mayor. She survived for many years, until at last, becoming destitute; she was taken to the workhouse where among other indignities she suffered that of being forcibly washed. This killed her.' (4)

Three scoundrels – Bardolph, Pistol and Nym – were all identifiable characters: Drinky Drinkwater, a renowned drunk and summertime vagrant spent his winters in Tewkesbury's workhouse and revelled in the notoriety the book afforded him. He regularly accosted the author for the price of a drink for daring to blacken his character, and Moore was always willing to oblige, regarding it a small price to pay. Drinky's fellow rogues, only known as Kennedy and Brown, had not survived. Together, the trio had spent their between-war days abusing authority, boozing, fighting, thieving and poaching, and once appeared before the magistrates for attempting to remove the War Memorial plinth from the Cross in the town centre.

While he may have thinly disguised the identity of some characters, John Moore did not attempt to conceal the effect many had had upon his formative years and genuinely harboured a belief that the stories fulfilled a need in post-war Britain:

> 'All the characters seemed real enough to me when I was writing them; and each owes something to a person or persons who walked the streets of Elmbury, and it should be remembered that they were written at the time of post-war frustrations, rationing and shortages, when for most of us the mood was somewhat anarchic in reaction against the disciplines and ardour of a long war. Homesickness and danger, the uncertainty of survival – and finally a sort of bewilderment that after all we had survived – had sharpened our memories and deepened our love for the hometown or village. Coming home to Tewkesbury I recollected and rediscovered a democracy of free men who were also funny men; their quirks, foibles, oddities and eccentricities unashamedly displayed with joy and thankfulness – with relief and deep affection I crowded them into these tales.' (5)

However popular and successful it was, *Portrait of Elmbury* did not please everyone. Simon & Schuster, the American publishers, objected to provocative passages about a Jew, and a few sentences about the Irish generated a storm of protest from several quarters:

> 'About a hundred Irishmen came to town. The pleasant, unfamiliar brogue of County Cork introduced a new gaiety into our streets; its owners brought to Elmbury also the filth, the fights and the squalor which accompany Irishmen wherever they go upon the face of the earth.' (6)

That passage certainly offended Father Moncrief, Tewkesbury's Catholic priest:

> 'Your generalisation could have been offset by the briefest allusion to constructive achievement; the building of the army depot at Aschurch, laying the pipeline through the length of Gloucestershire, erection of clean dwelling houses – all monuments to Irish sweated labour.' (7)

Stella Chapman, an Australian reader of Irish descent, also took the author to task:

> 'Your unhappy reference in so bitter a strain to the Irish, which my tolerance of all people makes me try hard to push into the background of my mind.' (8)

A further letter from the southern hemisphere left Moore in no doubt he had committed a serious error of judgement:

> 'I have just finished reading *Portrait of Elmbury.* I enjoyed it very much, except for one paragraph. I first wrote you a letter couched in mild terms. Being a sportsman, you would understand when I say it was the first barrel. I changed my mind and I am now going to give you both barrels at once. Pay attention Mr. Moore.

> 'My father was an Irishman. There was no filth about him and there are many like him left in Ireland. Thousands downed tools and went in a hurry when your country called in 1914. Too many of them are now asleep in foreign fields, but that did not deter their sons and grandsons going in their tens of thousands when your country called again. No filth and squalor accompanied them, but fight – yes – plenty.' (9)

Jack O'Brien, a veteran of both World Wars and one of the finest All-Blacks ever to grace a rugby field, took serious offence that required immediate mediation. Whatever Moore wrote in reply does not survive, but the result was a reconciliation that led to frequent correspondence and a sincere friendship.

> 'The more I know about you fellows, the less I understand. I merely fight for a principal. When you come to New Zealand, I hope it may be my pleasure to blow the froth off a couple with you. I am taking the liberty of forwarding you a food parcel, so that your Australian girl may cook up something.' (10)

The pair never met, although the exchanges of letters, books and food parcels continued until O'Brien's death from cancer in 1957.

Portrait of Elmbury brought a great deal of personal publicity: feature writers told of Moore's whirlwind romance and marriage to Lucile which, in one instance, resulted in unwelcome correspondence. Lucile's pre-war friend, Gerhard Stamer, read one such article. The German submariner was about to spend an eighth Christmas in captivity since being taken a prisoner of war when his U-boat sank off Land's End in September 1939, during an attempt to rescue the shipwrecked crew of a Greek freighter. Stamer spent the majority of the war in Canadian prison camps until, repatriated to England in 1946, he sought friendship and relief from loneliness by writing to

Lucile, after recognising her photograph in the magazine. His unsolicited approach did not find favour with John, who remained stubbornly prejudiced against his former enemy and in no mood for any form of reconciliation. He forbade contact between the former friends and it was not until after his death twenty years later that Lucile was able to visit Stamer and his wife in Germany.

'The bus put me down at the corner, and I walked towards the village along a winding lane. It was five years I had been away; and now after those five years of war and wandering I came back to my own land and my own people.' (11)

Moore cleared his desk at the Admiralty on 4 December, 1945, collecting his demob suit and discharge papers before returning home for good.

> 'In Gloucestershire's vale, made up of small farms and small fields with various and haphazard cultivations. Homely, unspectacular, neither too rich nor too poor. My people are like that too. Now the long episode was done, and we picked up the broken threads. It was easy to do that in the Fox and Hounds. We made up a four. We'd played our last game in August 1939 and now we played again, and I was happy and proud to be back with my own people, who have hard common sense in their heads and poetry in their hearts, who are patient and uncomplaining, and who are so much wiser than they seem.' (12)

He was no longer the carefree bachelor who six years earlier ventured to war on a surge of patriotism, but an ex-serviceman with an outlook on life changed by experiences of active service, loss of many friends and brushes with death. He returned to civilian life a much wiser, married man who could no longer think only of himself.

On New Year's Eve, he and Lucile dined with friends to celebrate a new beginning:

> 'I drank half-a-bottle of port, on top of claret and gin. And then we saw the New Year in at The Railway. Jack Turner, an admirable host, played a game called "Sing, Say or Pay." Everyone there, about 30, had to sing a song or tell a tale or contribute to the children's fund. I suppressed a desire to sing without difficulty and gave my imitation of Winston.' (13)

The following morning he visited another pub in the village, where he joined a group of railway workers. Their talk was about the new age of socialism and industrial nationalisation.

> ' "We've gone to work for a new boss today," they said. Their hopes for the success of nationalised transport very soon are sensible. They don't expect miracles but say that the chaps'll work better feeling it's their own show.' (14)

As a committed socialist, his own enthusiasm for the new order echoed their sentiments, but after several subsequent years of food rationing, power cuts and industrial unrest, he would become disillusioned.

Moore made his own fresh start with a new book. After the success of *Portrait of Elmbury* Collins had pressed him for more of the same and he got down to work immediately after leaving the Navy. *Brensham Village* was finished by the spring of 1946 and, reaching the bookshops in time for Christmas, equalled the sales of its predecessor. The thinly disguised locations were Bredon and the hill of the same name known locally as the 'Mother of the Cotswolds'. The characters were again drawn from people he knew – Joe Trentfield, licensee of the Horse Narrow could not be mistaken for any other than Jack Tyack at the Fox and Hounds – although most others were composites and not so readily identifiable. Once again, it was pure nostalgia about a way of life destroyed by the war years, perfectly portraying the countryside of that lost era, with the whiff of plants and animals on the breeze, and the crack of leather against willow from village greens.

> 'The apple blossom came out, and the willows put on their young green. The first cuckoo arrived and started calling from the adjacent meadow … there were cuckooflowers in this meadow too, a silver lilac carpet of them. Lapwings had their nests there and sometimes we found the mottled eggs.
>
> 'The whole of the vale and lower slopes of the hill were buried beneath a vast snowdrift of petals. As a rule the effect, as you look down on the flowering vale, is that of a lace curtain stretched loosely over it; for the plum blossoms are very small and even though they be multitudinous the leafless sepia twigs still show among them. However, in this season of unparalleled prodigality I had the impression not of a lace curtain, but of foam and lather, of curds overflowing a dish of cream. It was the loveliest June day you could possibly imagine, a day of blue and green and gold, and of light breezes, gilly-flower scented, and lullaby sounds of bees, wood pigeons and far away cuckoos. The sky was immaculate, hedge-sparrow egg blue; the mowing grass rippled in all the water meadows along the river, and like green foam were the leafy orchards on the lower slopes of the hill. Buttercups along the un-mown edge of our ground were a frieze of gold which gilded white cricket boots and the turn-ups of flannel trousers.' (15)

John Moore's cricket sequences could have been written by one of the sport's greatest writers, Neville Cardus:

'A cover drive flowed like a slow river with lovely lazy grace – the glance to leg as casual as an impertinent aside during a serious conversation – a glorious pull off middle stump like a laughing challenge to the Gods.' (16)

An annual match with a rival village, and the added handicap of a biased one-eyed umpire, is instantly recognisable to anyone who has spent a summer's day on a cow patch mown for the occasion:

'We minded very much who won. And especially we should mind if we were defeated by Woody Bourton who were known to us as Bloody Bourton. They had beaten us (or, as some said, their umpire had beaten us) the previous year and we thirsted for revenge.' (17)

There was, however, one error in the description that Moore lived to regret. Andrew Irvine, a retired classics master who read publishers' proofs and, being unable to ignore mistakes when reading for pleasure, wrote about a miscalculation of a bowling analysis in *Brensham Village*. There were, he said, several other inaccuracies:

'Coltsfoot flowers in February, not March – There are misquotations of Virgil and many instances of slipshod punctuation – I rebel at the omission of the comma before but and for etc – please take more care.' (18)

John Moore made a mistake in not taking him seriously:

'About the omission of commas; I have only one principle about punctuation and that is I say every sentence to myself as I write it in the way that I should like it to be read; and the punctuation marks represent, as it were, pauses of a different length according to the

> symbol used. I don't always think a pause comes before a conditional part of the sentence and if I don't think there should be a pause I don't put a comma ... And as for the cricket scores, I never was any good at the mathematics.' (19)

Such a Cavalier attitude did not meet with approval and, to Moore's increasing irritation Irvine continued to scrutinise his subsequent publications, eventually adding insult to injury by sending a signed copy of his own autobiography, *Sixty Years at School*, in which he wrote:

> 'I made friends with that delightful writer John Moore, whose *Brensham Village* contains a cricket match that deserves to become a classic. I wrote and asked him if he had yet noticed that the wrong number of wickets fell and the totals didn't work out right. It so happened that a reprint was imminent, and I offered so many corrections that in due course a copy of the new edition reached me with a charming inscription addressed to the "part author". The same writer asked me if I would read the proofs of his longest and most ambitious novel. It was an afterthought; unfortunately just too late for the first issue of a book which certainly needed vetting.' (20)

Moore privately exorcised his fury at such patronising pomposity by writing in his journal:

> 'That Irvine! He really is an awful old man. When he retired he greatly missed correcting pupils' examination papers and ever since then has occupied himself in correcting my books.' (21)

Brensham Village added to Moore's reputation as a popular writer and his agent had no problem in placing anything he wrote.

He was in demand as a reviewer, newspaper columnist and broadcaster; but success also brought some unfortunate consequences. He tried to follow the lifestyle of rural gentleman author before building a sufficient capital base to finance such an existence and spent every penny he made. Lucile opened a bookshop in Tewkesbury to supplement their income, but the venture struggled to survive and its only material advantage was to provide Moore with the storyline for his novel *Dance and Skylark*.

> 'It is pleasant to have a bookshop wife, because she provides a free library. It also keeps me with a sense of proportion, in that it teaches me the ups and downs of public favour and reminds me that the best seller of today is often the junk of tomorrow. Conversely, an author who didn't sell a thousand in his lifetime may become a collector's item at enormous cost.
>
> 'People also say it is a jolly good arrangement – you write books and she sells them – but it is not like that. She is a second-hand bookseller, trading mainly in first editions. And both our trades depend on this damnable rationing – if paper is plentiful my books sell – if there is a shortage her sales go up.' (22)

The business closed after four unsuccessful years.

> 'We gave up because of the embarrassment involved in making offers for books which owners, many of whom we knew, thought were worth a fortune. We sometimes bought out of sheer pity and the owners would go away convinced that all booksellers were crooks and that we would probably re-sell their book at an enormous profit.' (23)

'My people have poetry in their hearts and dreams in their heads – and, for much of the time, what feels like half the West Midlands on their boots.' (24)

The Blue Field, published in 1948, completed John Moore's famous trilogy about life in the Cotswolds. In highlighting a yeoman's bloody-minded independence, he employed earthy humour and a mixture of nostalgia, morning mist and birdsong to spin the tale of farmer Hart's resistance to a petty bureaucracy, which seeks to dictate what crops he would grow on his own land:

> 'On a day in late July, if you had stood on Bredon Hill and looked down the furzy slope towards the village you might have seen a remarkable spectacle. In the middle of the far distance, a seven-acre field had suddenly become tinctured with the colour of Mediterranean skies. One day there was a faint azure mist upon the field, like smoke from a squitch fire. Next morning when the sun came up a cerulean carpet covered it. We almost caught our breath, for although farmers with their seasonal rotations paint the land in many colours, blue is not one of them. And this particular shade of blue was something we had never seen in our countryside before. It made an extraordinary contrast with the remainder of the hillside.
>
> ' "I am wondering," said Mr Chorlton, "whether perhaps this is the kind of trivial gesture which begins big rows." ' (25)

Success followed for this further book of rustic anecdotes; it sold to thousands yearning relief from regulation, rationing and conscription. Hart's battle with authority was a perfect balm to sooth those frustrations and earned the author many admirers. The distinguished advocate Norman Birkett, reviewing for *The Sunday Times,* described Moore as the most successful country writer of his time, and regarded *The Blue Field* as a remarkable transcription of village life, told with wisdom, humanity, kindliness, humour and insight.

A young New Zealander also had good reason to empathise with William Hart: Torch Campbell wanted to read *The Blue Field,* but;

> 'Our piddling little bureaucratic officialdom won't let me get the dollars to send to your publishers in America, and I'm aware that it's not quite the thing for a lady to write to an author and ask for a gift of his book, but that's what I'm doing. I'd like to pay you in the black market way. If you write and tell me the size of your feet and the colour you like best, I'll knit you some socks made from New Zealand wool. Will you answer – Let's 'andle – or will you say No?' (26)

It was fair deal and an exchange of books and socks continued for some years.

The Blue Field was Moore's last full-length book for some time. Instead, he temporarily abandoned the disciplined regime of an author and enjoyed himself writing profitably for magazines and newspapers and extending his broadcasting career. The theatre, Savile, fishing, shooting and cricket were principal distractions; he even formed his own cricket team so that he could be sure of a game!

> 'Looking back on my cricketing career – the astonishing thing seems to be how I managed to stay so bad while playing so much. I used to dream of playing for England. All boys do. It's always the same sort of dream. If you're a batsman you save the side with a last wicket stand, and if you're a wicket keeper, as I claim to be, you take three marathon catches and stump the Aussie skipper. Oh, I saw it all so clearly in my dream.
>
> 'My wicket keeping does improve as I grow older. I concede fewer byes and have come to the

> conclusion this is a matter of sheer breadth. After every game nowadays I count up the bruises about my midriff; each one, I tell myself, represents four runs saved.' (27)

He readily settled into this comfortable existence, rising early to organise his correspondence and writing until noon. A lunchtime walk to the pub and leisurely afternoon preceded another evening session with his pen and a second visit of the day to the Fox and Hounds with Lucile. The only break with that routine was to fulfil the radio engagements that gradually took more of his time. He began regular broadcasting after an approach from BBC Midland talks' editor, Paul Humphreys, who had recalled Moore's pre-war nature talks when reading *Portrait of Elmbury*. He auditioned successfully and became a contributor to two topical programmes – *Sunday Out* and *Country Lover* – joining other well-known personalities such as Freddie Grizewood, Phil Drabble, Denys Watkins-Pitchford, Geoffrey Bright and C.V.Hancock. They provided popular weekend family listening for almost ten years before being eclipsed by the burgeoning medium of television. Every programme had an air of spontaneous gaiety engendered by the group of like-minded colleagues who set out to explore a different rural location each week. They arrived at a chosen hostelry on Friday evening to plan content and spent the following day researching and recording their individual topics. Moore introduced a certain individuality to his contributions by travelling the countryside on horseback.

> 'The BBC hired me a horse when we visited a village in the Dukeries. The owner had corned it up for a week and as soon as I saw him, I knew I was in for trouble. Of course, he bucked me off, I landed badly and a broken bone poked through the skin of my arm. The only consolation was that I spent three days in Nottingham hospital, where the nurses are all as

> beautiful as film stars, but have much kindlier natures. I do not propose to ride a horse again unless I am somewhere handy to Nottingham!' (28)

Paul Humphreys always marvelled at John's uncanny empathy with animals and his ability to describe their characteristics in human terms, examples of which abound in his broadcasts and writing:

> 'There was a little Siamese we called Mishy, whom we came near to possessing ... She was very small, a fairy-cat almost, who would dance the steps of ballet dancers to herself daintily, and whose strange conceit it was to steal hair-curlers and pipe cleaners, which she would carry around in her mouth and hide in secret places.
>
> 'But apart from this quaint fancy she was a sedate cat, and very gentle, and her paws were always soft in play. Even in courtship, she was silent, and when she had kittens it was always a surprise to us, and I think a surprise to her too. They were always black kittens and, by Siamese standards, illegitimate.
>
> 'I said she was gentle, and so she was at all times save when she had these kittens and there were dogs about. Then she became a spitting fury and her tail fluffed out into a witch's broom.' (29)

> 'I no longer have much regard for the gundogs of my youth – all doleful eyes, slobbering mouth and unquestioning obedience. I would prefer an animal of some spirit and individuality – something with the skill and individuality of a gypsy lurcher.
>
> 'My friend Brian Vesey Fitzgerald, the editor of The Field, is an expert of both dogs and gypsies. He tells me I should aim for a true lurcher (Bedlington terrier/Greyhound cross); not a mongrelly looking

> animal of Greyhound appearance. The trouble is that lurchers bred by gypsies are very rarely for sale to other than gypsies, but he knows the chief breeders, James Arigho, Manaseh Burton, Noah Boswell and Amos Locke.
>
> 'Manaseh Burton may have a spare one soon and he will be travelling through Evesham in late April on his annual migration to the New Forest. Brian wonders whether to give him my address and suggest he calls, but this may encourage an annual visit and may not go down too well with neighbours (or Lucile)!' (30)

Moore also made a significant contribution as a literary reviewer and recorded many of his opinions in his journal.

> 'In my literary appetite, I think I am a somewhat coarse fellow. If you can see what I mean, I like a whacking great steak and chips, with a pint or two of beer, rather than some little fiddling concoction that has to be matched with just the right sort of white wine.'
>
> 'The most exciting thing that can happen to a reviewer, next to receiving, unheralded out of the blue, a blazing masterpiece – and that is likely to happen once in fifty years – the most exciting thing is to read a really good first novel. Even that's pretty rare; for writing is a difficult trade that has to be learned the hard way by trial and error, and as a rule novelists don't spring fully armed into the world.'
>
> 'Young writers generally begin their career by writing poetry, which is very necessary and proper, because a young writer who doesn't believe himself to be an inspired poet had better not write at all. However, they soon get over the poetry stage as a rule, and the next thing they try their hand at is almost always a short story. This is odd because the short story is

> probably the most difficult form in the whole writing repertory. You've got to have a lot of experience in your craft before you can handle it confidently. You must have learned how to write with economy and you must know how to select – what to put in and what to leave out – which is one of the most tricky parts of the writer's trade. A novel can be quite untidy and loosely constructed, and still be a good and even a great novel – for example Pickwick Papers or Tristram Shandy. But a short story has to be as strict as a sonnet.'
>
> 'In the late Thirties, and again immediately after the war, I did a lot of reviewing, and as time went by I became less eager to tackle the novels because so many bored me stiff. In certain respects, the standards were pretty high; most of their authors wrote excellent prose ... the characters were well conceived; the dialogue was often crisp and sometimes witty. There was, however, one thing wrong with seven-tenths of those novels. Their authors omitted to tell a story. Surely, there has never been a time when so many of our good writers were writing clever books about nothing. If you read only the novels of what I suppose I must loosely call the high-brows – you would be tempted to believe that the swift and shining streams of story telling had dried up at its source, that there were no more tales in the world to be told.' (31)

He could be infuriatingly self-opinionated and patronising, but was invariably sympathetic to new writers and never influenced by the reputations of established figures. He discovered *The Day of the Triffids* by John Wyndham:

> 'The author is a new man of literature. The immensely fertile and gloriously speculative mind of HG Wells produced few more exciting inventions than

> this book. To read it is an experience rather like, I should think, the first reading of *The Time Machine* when it came out in 1895.' (32)

Of C.P.Snow's *The Masters,* he wrote -

> 'He's a fine novelist. I think he may come to be considered a great one.' (33)

In addition, he unhesitatingly criticised Hemingway's *Across the River and into the Trees:*

> 'I wish it had never been published. One of a mere handful of living novelists with an international reputation. I greatly admire him, but this book is a lapse – it is a complete disaster. If literature, like other professions, has its code of honour and integrity, then I think Mr Hemingway has betrayed it.' (34)

However, *The Old Man and the Sea* found favour:

> 'Strangely beautiful. Written with simplicity. Hemingway has not always, lately, touched the heights; but when he is at the top of his form few storytellers, English or American, can come near him. In this sad, quiet tale he is at the very top of that form.' (35)

Moore's relaxed avuncular radio manner, however, did not readily transfer to television; as he wrote of his first appearance as presenter of *The Bookman,* he was not at ease in front of the camera:

> 'After ten "takes" they managed to get a few minutes of suitable chat with the young lady I was interviewing. Afterwards I gave her a copy of one of my books and was moved to write my thanks to her in a

> shaky hand, and added that she had taken part in my first and probably last television appearance!' (36)

He did not appear on the small screen again until 1962 when, after introducing five editions of *Eye on the Countryside* for Central TV, he abandoned any idea of a television career. He was, however, an impressive orator and the British Transport film unit commissioned him to write and narrate the scripts for two productions: *Heart of England* and *The England of Elizabeth*. Both were worthy pieces of descriptive prose, and the première of the former at the Vienna film festival led to an invitation from a BBC documentary unit:

> 'The BBC rang me up and asked me if I would like to write a feature programme about Dartmoor and I had to confess that it happened to be one of the few parts of England which I hardly knew at all.
>
> 'This turned out to be an advantage in a way, because I had a sense of adventure, as soon as I took my first step away from the main road. I started off with a preconceived disbelief in almost all the travellers' tales I have heard about the place; and ultimately discovered most of them to be true.
>
> 'I stayed on the moor for a fortnight and explored it, first by car, then by pony and finally on foot. The November mists persisted and in fact, I lost myself almost every day. I was a bit ashamed until I met two men from the Royal Marines who were completely lost in the course of an exercise. A place that could lose the Royal Marines could lose anybody.
>
> 'The first thing that impressed me about the moor was its immense loneliness. I was alone with the Galloway cattle, the ponies, the horned Scotch sheep, and the buzzards mewing like cats high above the Tors.
>
> 'The next thing that struck me was how slight was the impact which man had made upon the moor.

> Dartmoor is still much the same as it was when the bronze-age people wandered over it.
>
> 'So when I came home I wrote of Dartmoor as I saw it; as the last great wilderness which in this tame polite countryside of ours still holds out against man.' (37)

The actual making of *The Last Wilderness,* however, did not convince Moore that it was an experience worth repeating:

> 'In many ways it is a hateful occupation, subject to innumerable delays. One of our girls lost the head handkerchief, which she'd been wearing for two days and until she found it tucked in the flap of her saddle we were held up. Apparently, one is always running up against these difficulties of continuity. One cannot have a wristlet watch shot in one scene at 1 o'clock and the next 6 o'clock when the second is set only half an hour later.
>
> 'We found that Dartmoor mist produced by the Royal Marine smoke bombs was better than that supplied by the Almighty – so we used it all the time. We also found that the Tavistock fire brigade provided us with better and more reliable rain as well, so they tagged along wherever we went.
>
> 'We hired a complete fox-hunt with hounds and followers for £20 to the hunt servants' benevolent fund, and convicts were provided free by the prison – though we had to shoot them from behind, and if we needed a close up we had an actor personally dressed by the Governor.
>
> 'Among our various properties were the skeleton of a sheep from a museum, although nature provided an abundance of better ones, and two live adders from a pet shop in London. These, alas, we had to kill after they had played their parts, because it was felt that to liberate adders on Dartmoor might endanger children.

> No-one took into account that there are hundreds of adders there already!' (38)

He did court the film industry for work as a scriptwriter, trailing around Herefordshire hop-fields behind a producer with ideas for a romantic comedy, but nothing came of it apart from the germ of an idea for one of his most successful novels. 'I have wasted ten months of my life on a sterile and still born film,' he told A.D.Peters, who advised him to stick to books.

'This year, for the first time in my life, I possess a garden of my own. Some exciting things are beginning to come up in the flowerbeds. I am rather disturbed to find that I have a disposition to boast inordinately about them.' (39)

'Country Column' appeared in the *Birmingham Evening Mail* for the first time in January 1949. It was providential that the new source of income should coincide with a move to a substantial house in the village of Kemerton, barely a mile from Bredon. Its purchase had taken every penny he possessed.

> 'I had to do a lot of bread and butter writing and broadcasting as well as the books; proof reading for Dents at £3 a book and scores of reviews for the Observer.' (40)

The new house, expensive cars and extravagant living consumed the small fortune earned by his post-war successes, and he therefore grasped with both hands the opportunity to write a regular newspaper feature for ten guineas a week. He became a popular contributor for twenty years, writing almost a thousand consecutive articles that, in a light, conversational and sometimes provocative manner, introduced a largely urban audience to rural England.

He sought to educate and entertain, campaigning unashamedly for a better understanding of the rural economy and the need to conserve the countryside and its way of life for the benefit of everyone. Sometimes, however, he miscalculated the likely reaction to a story.

> 'A half wild stray tom cat descended upon the household and is terrorising all the inhabitants, feline and otherwise. For our part we loathe the sight of him – he walked into our house as if it were his own, stinks the place out, misbehaves everywhere.' (41)

A woman from the centre of Birmingham offered the villain a home: 'don't send him by train – are you on a bus route – if so, I will collect him.' Moore's reply that a feral cat would be unlikely to settle to urban domesticity could not dissuade her and several letters to the editor followed, berating the author's inhumane attitude.

> 'It was meant to be a light hearted article. I never thought anybody would take me up about that bloody cat. The animal is still around – a revolting beast. The thought of capturing it, packing it and despatching it to Birmingham presents an awful proposition. It certainly couldn't be taken on a bus and unless held captive would be off just as soon as it arrived.' (42)

Another article intended as a light-hearted advertisement for the delights of Tewkesbury's annual Mop Fair brought more heartache.

> 'One side show was worth anybody's sixpence. It advertised striptease and snakes; and sure enough in a kind of pit, there sat somewhat wanly, on this very cold evening, a lady well past her blooming youth with very few clothes on. Crawling over her, and wrapped about her arms and neck, were no less than six pythons.

They delighted me and curiously enough, they seemed to delight the middle-aged lady in the bikini, for she fondled them lovingly with one hand, while with the other she munched a ham sandwich. Six pythons and striptease too! (43)

Unfortunately, a regular reader owned the booth.

'My sideshow – Chequitta – The Amazing Snake Charmer featured at Tewkesbury Mop, and is the only snake show on the road this year. It did not display a notice about striptease; the lady was not dressed in a bikini – instead she wore a full one-piece costume and a sarong. It is somewhat ungallant to infer that a forty year old lady is a relic, particularly as Chequitta is my wife.' (44)

The editor, fearing an action for defamation, demanded an immediate apology and a contrite Moore wrote:

'What pitfalls and gins do beset the path of those of us who write for the papers. I was careful to avoid any identification and it is most unfortunate that your snake show is the only one on the road. Any public apology would only draw further attention to your identity. I will take the opportunity to call on you and buy you a beer, but I hope to goodness I don't meet your wife! I am truly sorry if I inadvertently caused her distress.' (45)

Moore thought his urban readership largely misunderstood the purpose of hunting with hounds and continually returned to the subject during his time with the paper. Steeped in family hunting tradition – with a sister who devoted her whole life to the sport – he always remained a supporter of the practicalities and ethics of the chase.

> 'It is possible that the House of Commons will debate more passionately about blood sports than it did about Palestine. This will be extremely disconcerting to foreigners. Neither the Russians nor Americans find it easy to understand our political habit of fighting like cats and dogs about what I will call moral issues, while presenting a spectacle of astonishing unanimity in the face of great crises.
>
> 'I should like to make one comment which has nothing to do with the pros and cons of hunting. I used to hunt; I no longer do so; and on the whole, I deplore the attitude of people whose chief interest is killing foxes. But much more than that I deplore the attitude of people who want to stop others doing things which they themselves disapprove of.
>
> 'There is a case for the humane aspects of fox culling – only the old, infirm and diseased are killed – the fit escape. Those killed by hounds are spared the terror, decrepitude and starvation of illness or old age. They are despatched in seconds and none get away injured to die the slow death of those not cleanly shot, trapped or poisoned. Imagine the horror of lying in a dark lair in the throes of gangrene, the gripes of poison, the agony of a leg caught in a snare or waiting in a trap for the dawn that brings the man with a gun to execute the *coup de grace* ... Foxes are good pest control officers – we need to accommodate their presence to maintain a balance among voles, rats, frogs, beetles and rabbits.' (46)

In recent years parliament has exercised those self-same arguments during two hundred hours spent debating the abolition of hunting with hounds, and less than a dozen committing the United Kingdom to a war! Whenever Moore pronounced what he regarded as balanced arguments he invariably received hostile correspondence, sometimes accompanied by threats of violence. However, he never shied away from what he believed to be right, and insisted on forcefully putting his view.

> 'Dear Hunt Saboteur – I am wholly in favour of fox-hunting; but because I believe in democracy I'd fight hard for your right to protest against it if any despot should seek to take that right from you.
>
> 'Do you believe in democracy by the way? If so, can you honestly maintain that it could exist for very long if a lot of people like you took it upon themselves to interfere physically with the perfectly legal pastime of other people just because they happen to disapprove of them?
>
> 'Is the opponent of boxing justified in jumping into the boxing ring? Would, for example, country dwellers, who suffer disturbed weekends by car rallies, be justified in blocking off our roads with tractors, scattering nails etc; opponents of games on the Sabbath digging up pitches; prudes about bathing costumes spreading oil on beaches?
>
> 'You say only idiots and insensitive oafs really find pleasure in foxhunting. But that's just what I say about people who go to watch soccer matches.
>
> 'If you believe in democracy you must obey the rules of democracy. Argue, publish your pictures and thoughts, and march to the meet with your banners. I'd gladly go to prison for your right to do so. But don't be so damnably arrogant and utterly undemocratic as to believe you have a right to spoil a legitimate activity because you happen not to approve.' (47)

On one occasion, he offended many by comments made against a more popular sport that he himself had enjoyed since schooldays, and which had brought him considerable financial and professional advantage:

> 'Coarse fishing – a blood sport which counts its supporters by the million and compares unfavourably to the hunter with hounds who despatches his quarry with immediate finality. Fish, played at the end of a line before being landed in an alien element or escaping with hooks remaining in lip or throat, or a mouthful of artificial six-barbed lure.
>
> 'Only idiots believe that fish do not feel pain, and some are caught again and again in agony.
>
> 'The hunt protestor demonstrates, not for the benefit of the fox, but to make a social point of hatred against certain human beings, their manners, speech, conventions and traditions.
>
> 'If you are motivated by something other than a chip on your shoulder, surely you should risk a ducking by carrying your banner to a fishing match – I dare you to try it.' (48)

The implied suggestion of cruelty incensed those well aware of his devotion to the sport, and the largest collective of anglers in the country – the Birmingham Angling Association – roundly accused him of hypocrisy. Once again, he was obliged to pen a conciliatory note:

> 'I am of course a fisherman, and have been all my life. I fish for the pot and quickly kill everything I catch. But, however much I have difficulty understanding you people who sit for hours in the cold and rain watching a float to disappear beneath the surface and return whatever you catch, I will always defend your rights to do so.' (49)

The occasional spats did not detract from the column's overall popularity and Moore was always genuinely grateful for the support given by readers to his numerous campaigns over conservation issues. Preservation of the natural environment had been of particular concern since roaming the Malvern Hills in his schooldays and deepened further when he personally experienced the effects of economic depression, consequences of intensive farming and climate change upon the countryside. He wrote about changes on the fertile slopes of Bredon Hill: removal of hedgerows to facilitate larger machinery; stubble burning and irresponsible application of chemicals – all playing a part in destroying natural habitats and soil structures nurtured over previous centuries.

> 'How my uncle would stand and stare. Combine harvesters roving immature prairies where once was the patchwork of English fields. Crop rotation has disappeared, instead there is barley year after year, achieved by adding nitrogen to the soil – no farmer can afford the old practice of leaving land fallow to rest.
>
> The whole male population of my village would not now be sufficient to harvest by scythe one-tenth of the corn which now grows on Bredon Hill.' (50)

> 'There is a harvest gloom. No countryman has seen anything like it in living memory. Last year we had a wet summer; the hay crop was poor, as was the harvest. A wet winter followed and then a wet spring. Growers have been unable to prepare the ground for planting and we have starving livestock. All the food stocks are used up early and so are the reserves. We are so preoccupied with our difficulties that we scarcely noticed them seeping away.' (51)

His main concern was as a naturalist:

> 'My county council would like to see only grass growing on roadside verges. It says that hedge parsley is unsightly and poppies are weeds, and with other broad-leaved plants should be sprayed out by the use

of hormone weed-killers. What these technicians do not realise is that they are killing the last refuge for all living things now that farmers use so much of these chemicals. A weed is a beautiful plant growing in the wrong place, and a roadside verge is not the wrong place.

'What is the value of an English hedge-side? In spring, lacy umbels of hedge parsley with orange-tip butterflies exquisitely matching them, lesser stitchwort like new-laundered linen, milky primroses, buttercups and celandines. And in summer? Scarlet poppies, blue cornflowers, burnet-moths on flower heads and clover a-buzz with bees. And in autumn? Traveller's-Joy so rightly named, and coral-red berries of the wild arum.

'By destroying the roadside flowers we rob wild bees of one of their remaining sources of honey and pollen; and without the wild bees and certain flies the farmers' crops won't get fertilized.

'The chemists are very efficient executioners. They kill the farmers' foes alright, but they kill the farmers' friends as well. Organic phosphates kill bird and beast as well as insects. By this means, we wipe out still more of our friends. Real naturalists know about the inter-relation of creatures and the complicated equality of insects and plants. They know that one of the best ways to control a pest is to encourage the enemy of that pest. Naturalists like myself aren't a lot of obscurantist fuddy-duddies. We want to use science, but use it properly and not recklessly, carelessly, wantonly, ignorantly.

'These people do not realise that by burning a hundred acres of heath or destroying a wood to get rid of a few rabbits they destroy everything else – ground-nesting birds, voles, mice, shrews, uncommon plants. And no-one asks the advice of the ecologist

> before the flamethrowers and bulldozers move in. The lovely pattern of pastoral England is being destroyed by those who do not realise that it is a compromise between agricultural necessity and an acceptance that the pattern involves some co-existence with some things which compete with humans for food.' (52)

He was, however, aware that a balance was necessary between sentimentality and practicality.

> 'The rabbit, the rat and the pigeon must be controlled just as the black fly on your beans or the caterpillars on your cabbage. It is a question of degree, and it is also a question of method. Unless you take steps to defend yourself against these foes, you will be lucky if they leave you enough to live on. Let us take the rabbit plague of recent years. We do not always serve the cause of what kindly folk call "God's Creatures" by being sentimental about them, but that does not mean we have to be cruel.
>
> 'And in my opinion myxomatosis is not cruel. People who see rabbits dying of the disease are shocked, but have mostly never seen a rabbit in a gin trap – I have. Like all countrymen I have been tormented at night by the pitiful cries of rabbits in gins; I have seen my cat after she has been caught in one. So, I welcomed myxomatosis because its effect was to reduce the total of suffering. It killed off in one go about ninety-five per cent of the rabbit population; and that means, I hope that the gin which tortured perhaps twenty per cent of rabbits every year will be unnecessary.' (53)

Moreover, as a pragmatist, he always welcomed small optimistic indicators for the future:

> 'Nature reserves of wide verges at the side of motorways and arterial roads have been unwittingly constructed by man. They will be undisturbed and unspoilt areas of natural cultivation into which wildlife will settle once used to the distraction of unremitting traffic noise. In twenty years a census of wildlife; kestrels, foxes, frogs, wrens, tree-creepers, owls, living within four miles of Birmingham city centre will astound.' (54)

John Moore conducted a long campaign against despoilment of the countryside by those motivated by profit margins and a careless disregard for ecological structures. Many loyal readers supported his views and together they harried officialdom into action. Eventual achievements included sympathetic management of rural roadside vegetation, controls in the use of harmful pesticides, preservation of hedgerows, trees, wetlands and wildlife habitats, and prevention of stubble burning.

Chapter 6

Mixed Fortunes – 1951-58

'I was at first doubtful and indeed somewhat appalled. It had never occurred to me that a whole week of talks and similar solemnities would even fill half the big Town Hall. Moreover, there had never been such a thing as a purely literary festival in Britain before.' [(1)]

Cheltenham's renowned Festival of Contemporary Literature was the brainchild of a town clerk with a desire to lift the cultural malaise of post-war years. John Moore's previous experience as organiser of Tewkesbury Festival brought him to mind as a consultant, although his initial reaction was less than enthusiastic. A purely literary festival was an innovation and he shared the view of well-known author J.B.Priestley, who, when also asked for an opinion, said that literature is something personal between writer and reader, unlike the communal arts of music and drama. Presumably, the immediate success of the new concept and the speed with which it developed surprised both.

After considerable persuasion, Moore assisted with the first venture and, thereafter, found himself tied to an annual event that would occupy a great deal of his time over several years. He propositioned all his contacts at the Savile club to fill the initial programme and persuaded an old Fleet Air Arm colleague and native of the town, a somewhat reluctant Ralph Richardson, to perform the opening ceremony in October 1949.

Tongue-in-cheek, Richardson demanded that his host write a 'brilliant speech' for his use and provide a briefing on every dot and comma. He said he wished to say some charming things about a town he hardly remembered, but as an inadequate public speaker did not wish to bore an audience for more than ten minutes! In the event his presentation was perfect: he compiled his own address and captivated everyone with charm, wit and theatrical presence. Compton Mackenzie volunteered to speak about the contemporary novel; Ivor Brown discussed words; Arthur Bryant defined the English national character and Cecil Day Lewis recited his own verse. A newcomer, Emma Smith, introduced her prize-winning book, *Maidens' Trip* about life working on canal barges during wartime and, as a finale, Joyce Grenfell and Stephen Potter debated the glory of literature.

To everyone's surprise, the week attracted an audience of seven thousand, and brought substantial commercial benefit to the town. The staged events returned a small profit, encouraging the Town Council to solicit Moore's help for another year. As an incentive he was appointed a vice-president of the Cheltenham Arts Festival, an honour only previously extended to the conductor Sir John Barbirolli. Success met with more success and for each of the ensuing four years Moore spent three months of his time voluntarily planning and supervising the event, eventually establishing it as a permanent feature in the town's cultural calendar. During that time he widened the programme to embrace all fields of literature, with talks or discussions about novels, poetry, biography, criticism, drama and scriptwriting. The demands became too much for Moore to shoulder alone, and in 1954 he was joined by a co-chairman, Colonel Robert Henriques, Cotswold landowner, farmer, author and former professional soldier who moved in influential literary circles.

The pair never had difficulty persuading speakers to attend in return for modest fees because most had books, poems or ideas to sell. There were exceptions and some proved difficult to accommodate. C.P.Snow refused to oppose his wife, the novelist Pamela Hansford Johnson, in a debate about contemporary literature, on grounds that they never argued about anything. John Betjeman baulked at the idea of participating in an Any Questions session or commenting upon what Moore had described as his light verse – as he did not think his verse was as light as all that, he said, and, furthermore, he did not like parlour games. He agreed to read his poetry or talk about Tennyson and, in a typical Betjemanesque aside, expressed pleasure at the proposed fee as he was well used to speaking to Women's Institutes for nothing! Regular speakers eagerly anticipated the generous hospitality provided by the co-chairmen, their house parties becoming a permanent feature of festival week. Cecil Day Lewis, C.S.Forester, Betjeman and Kingsley Amis were among many personalities who regularly accepted invitations to speak in return for good food and fine wine. Laurie Lee was one of the few to turn down an invitation; only because of domestic circumstances – his young daughter was like a good wine that would not travel – he and his wife had recently departed prematurely from other parties to allow households relief from her crying. He later accepted an invitation, but travelled alone to what he described as a party of the best kind, with 'guests singing in odd corners against each other like birds in a belfry'.

Some guests proved unreasonably temperamental. Gilbert Harding, to no-one's great surprise, drank to excess and his coarse language reduced Lucile to tears. Although never again invited by the festival committee, he subsequently chaired a live broadcast of 'Any Questions' for the BBC from the Town Hall and caused further unpleasantness by writing to the press about the poor standard of local hotels. It also proved unwise to invite another renowned toper to address a matinee audience of schoolchildren. Dylan Thomas, scruffily attired in a cigarette-ash and beer stained jacket, leered mischievously at a sea of innocent faces as John Moore watched nervously from the rear of the hall.

> 'I shall never forget the effect on Cheltenham Ladies' College of one of the more surprising poems which he chose to read us – it began – "As she was soaping her breasts in the bath ..."
>
> 'The girls in their sea-green uniforms were rippling with delight like the waves of the sea, and I remember how the disapproving backs of the mistresses rose up straight as ramrods.' (2)

During those first four years contented audiences listened to prominent personalities, but the repetitive format eventually reduced attendances. Moore, therefore, tried innovation by introducing a poetry competition in 1953, judged by Richard Church and Cecil Day Lewis. Peggy Ashcroft and John Laurie were engaged to read the winning entries on the final evening, but unfortunately the venture attracted widespread publicity for all the wrong reasons. The local newspaper dismissed as worthless a leaked entry by the racing driver, Stirling Moss and John Moore made matters worse by kicking up a fuss. Several prominent Gloucestershire residents made pompous issue in the press when the judges peremptorily rejected their efforts and a gallant colonel bristled with indignation when only awarded a consolation prize. An obsequious parson added a further farcical element by lending his support in the letters pages to a hopeless effort by a titled woman. The judges created further problems for themselves by taking an inordinately long time over their deliberations, finally declaring that there could be no overall winner as the best entry, a lengthy piece of blank verse, did not fall within the rules. However, 'Gloucestershire Exile' – by an unknown Sidney Knight – had so captured their imagination that Laurie insisted upon reading it at the gala evening.

Knight was born into poverty in the Cotswold village of Broadway in the latter years of the nineteenth century. He received little education and could neither read nor write when he joined the Royal Navy at the outbreak of the First World War. Discharged on medical grounds and unjustly denied a pension, he drifted around the world before settling in Johannesburg with a huge chip on his shoulder.

> 'The Lords Commissioners of the Immorality made me redundant after eight years' service. I reached the level of the park bench; cold, sick and hungry and too afraid to go home and face my family. For many of us down and outs the only warm place was the library and that is how I discovered books.' (3)

He educated himself and with dogged determination became a regular writer about South African political affairs for American magazines. His ambition was to write poetry, but increasingly frustrated by an inability to gain sponsorship he slid towards despair and bankruptcy.

Moore was also taken by 'Gloucestershire Exile,' and asked Knight's permission to publish it in pamphlet form and have John Laurie read it for the BBC's poetry programme. He knew nothing of the poet's personal circumstances and the manic tone of the reply shocked him.

> 'Your letter came just in time to stop me diving down the well. This Dark Continent is as dark as a sweep's arse. This country is doomed. I had a bad day today – these jockeys couldn't ride a clotheshorse. I have lived in grim poverty and I shall die in poverty, cursing the system that caused it – do you know a vacant almshouse?' (4)

Knight's despair, however satirical, touched Moore and began yet another supportive friendship by correspondence. Knight poured out his troubles in lengthy letters in which he railed against a literary establishment that would not give him a break. He did not always receive sympathy.

> 'You are always having a bang at what you think of the highbrows of literature and it is therefore a curious paradox that it is precisely these highbrows who think most highly of your work: the reason being that they are for the most part trained Men of Letters who can recognise the real thing when they see it. Now will you cease and just write?' (5)

That blunt message spawned *Cotswold Lad,* a vigorous evocative book about working class poverty and Knight's lifelong struggle against unattractive odds. Moore's enthusiastic reviews ensured its success and generated other gratefully acknowledged commissions.

> 'So the old horse has made the stable at last. I have struck a rich load in the US; 50 Bucks an article is real money. I am almost afraid to come home. I think I prefer my sweetheart Broadway at a distance. My beautiful hills cannot be ruined in my mind, but I should just like to see them once more. My God, we exiles have to pay a price.' (6)

Knight relapsed into melancholy soon afterwards without achieving his full potential as a sardonic writer. He died in Africa and never revisited his beloved Broadway.

In 1954 Lord David Cecil, Emma Smith and C.P.Snow judged the best debut novel of the year, but again things did not run smoothly when they failed to reach agreement and Snow resigned in a huff. Moore took his place and Brigid Brophy's *Hackenfeller's Ape* won the competition with Iris Murdoch's *Under the Net* in second place. The judges all rejected one of the great literary successes of the twentieth century, *Lord of the Flies* by future Nobel Laureate William Golding.

It seemed that any new initiative Moore devised would encounter difficulties when Norman Edwards, editor of *TV Mirror*, asked to judge entries submitted by aspiring television scriptwriters, struggled to cope with four thousand entries. Moore's hyperbolic advance publicity was undoubtedly to blame for the response.

> 'TV offers a new challenge. It brings the writer's character and innermost thoughts right inside the cottage, council house, suburban dwelling, and city flat or grand house. But where are the writers who through TV will perhaps make themselves, by reason of its universality, more widely known than perhaps even Kipling or Arnold Bennett or Hardy?' (7)

At considerable expense, a team of hastily recruited professional readers sifted through a welter of rubbish and found only two entries worthy of consideration. Record audiences enjoying a glittering array of speakers – Andre Maurois, Christopher Fry, Malcolm Muggeridge, A.G. Street, Lady Isobel Barnett and Marghanita Laski – could do nothing to recoup the unforeseen expense and the festival ran at an overall loss. The experience confirmed that the event had outgrown the best intentions of its amateur organisers and was in urgent need of sponsorship and professional management. The Town Council, insisting upon greater representation and budgetary control, forced the resignation of both Henriques and Moore.

The festival failed again in the following year and John Moore was persuaded to return in 1956 with a free rein. He used all his considerable influence to secure the best speakers and extended the programme to include debates and writers' workshops. Unfortunately, he did not arrest declining audiences and in 1961 financial losses compelled cancellation. Pessimists predicted that the event had probably run its course. Moore refused to accept defeat and battled tirelessly to secure additional finance and promote necessary changes to modernise the format. His personal contribution was to write his only theatrical production, contributing all profits from debut performances to festival funds.

The Elizabethans, a dramatised anthology performed by seven actors, used material from the time of the first Elizabeth and included poetry, prose and music by Shakespeare, Spenser, Ben Johnson, Donne and Marlowe. John Moore directed the first production in Cheltenham's Everyman Theatre, before taking it to the Theatre Royal at Windsor. In subsequent years, it became a set piece at RADA and still regularly appears as a minor theatrical piece. Fund-raising by a number of similarly committed festival supporters could not hope to meet the full costs of what had become a considerable financial undertaking, so Moore persuaded the governing committee to seek commercial and industrial sponsorship. He also recommended the salaried appointment of

Elizabeth Jane Howard, an emerging novelist and organiser of considerable intellect, as general manager.

Ms Howard brought new ideas and vigour to the proceedings and her 1962 festival was a great success. Unfortunately, she resigned immediately afterwards for personal reasons and John Moore was persuaded to return in 1963. He returned a profit, but the pressures involved on his declining health obliged him reluctantly to withdraw from further active participation. His resignation left a void and the festival lapsed until coming under new direction in 1965.

The annual event, which owes much to the original vision, enthusiasm and perseverance of John Moore, is still the largest literary festival in Europe.

'I have had three years of financial trouble with great arrears of income tax. I try not to worry. A new novel should put us right. I'm sure we'll get through.' (8)

John Moore's childhood of genteel poverty following the death of his father shaped a determination to reclaim the position in Gloucestershire society formerly enjoyed by his ancestors. The financial success of his three post-war books provided ample money to adopt a lifestyle in keeping with an aesthete and country squire, while the position of Festival Director and opportunity to mix with influential people enhanced his reputation.

The visitor's book from Kemerton Lodge bears witness to personalities who ate at his table: old friends – Ludovic Kennedy and Moira Shearer (Moore was godfather to their first child), Nicholas Monsarrat, Cecil Day Lewis, Graham Green and Dylan Thomas; companions from the Savile – Ralph Richardson, Arthur Bliss, C.S.Forester and John Betjeman; and local aristocrats – The Earls Baldwin and Beauchamp. Moreover, well-known actors from the RSC at Stratford graced every occasion. His cricket team prospered, and sporting Moore's personal colours, played annual fixtures against actors, literary societies, publishing houses and touring teams of gentlemen players.

He employed a full-time secretary; young ladies recruited from a nearby commercial college generally stayed with him until they married; treated as members of the family they spent more time as companions to Lucile and hostesses than working at a typewriter. The only other member of staff was an ancient gardener with whom John enjoyed a fractious relationship. Henry, a slave to the routine of the gardening year, waged a personal battle against weeds and insects and did not hold with his master's liking for unkempt patches where his enemies could flourish. In his traditional lights, lawns should be smooth and symmetrical, vegetables grown in straight lines and flowers and shrubs in orderly beds. He and John were continually at odds and it was usually Lucile's conciliatory interventions that prevented the old man downing tools. Occasionally John was able to take subtle revenge:

> 'Home brewed beer has a remarkable effect on the gardener. He does all manner of jobs he generally has no liking for. Then I pack him off on his bicycle with a couple of bottles and don't see him for days. I must be sure to make some more!' (9)

However, eventually this ideal life exacted a price. Since leaving the navy Moore had neglected his obligations to the Inland Revenue and a tax inspector finally caught up with him in 1953.

> 'I bought a very expensive house at the top of the market, and a new car on HP, and entered into all kinds of fearful commitment, and forgot about the income tax. Well, one doesn't exactly forget; but one thinks of it rather as one thinks of the Last Reckoning; a reminder but by no means a deterrent of sin, something that can be squared up in the end.' (10)

He could not meet the arrears and life became increasingly difficult. He sold the Jaguar and an old Vauxhall took its place;

Kemerton Lodge went on the market, but in the middle of all these difficulties, his sense of humour did not completely desert him. Receiving an invitation to address the Herefordshire National Savings Committee on the subject of thrift, he somewhat petulantly declined.

> 'I feel if anyone has any money left over after the Income Tax have got at it they have a right to spend it as they see fit. I should be the last person to encourage anyone to put it into National savings, where its true value is squandered by the government'. (11)

He also thought of becoming a tax exile:

> 'I need to recharge my batteries – I do not think an author should write about the same place for too long – I shall go abroad'. (12)

It was an idle threat and, when the house did not sell, he turned to his mother for help.

> 'We have tried so hard, but the value dropped. I should lose £2,500 and by the time I paid estate agents and lawyers I'd have nothing left and no roof over our heads. Money paid to building societies is in a way money put away, whereas money paid in rent just disappears.' (13)

Ina did not hesitate and advanced a loan from her meagre capital in a well intentioned, but futile gesture. Her selflessness did nothing to stave off an ultimatum.

> 'In the light of the previous history of this matter no further deferment can be permitted, and proceedings for recovery will commence for any amount remaining unpaid on 1st January, 1954.' (14)

The shame of bankruptcy loomed, necessitating humiliating admissions in order to buy time.

> 'It now appears unlikely that I can meet your demand, and I must therefore face the threat contained in your letter. I got behind with my Income Tax and other obligations. This was no doubt reprehensible, but was due less to mismanagement of personal finances than the failure of a film company, which owed me £750 and the fact that one of my novels was a "flop". Such chances are inseparable from the precarious profession of an author.
>
> 'I have paid some arrears of Income Tax and Surtax – a little over half my income (after tax) for the current year. I recite these facts in order to demonstrate that I have not merely "showed willing": I have in fact made every effort and sacrifice to recover from a heavy misfortune and to satisfy my debt to the Revenue.
>
> 'You must consider whether it would really serve the interests of the Revenue to take the step you have threatened, or whether you would consider the liquidation of the debt by monthly payments.' (15)

He earned a stay of execution, but it took years completely to recover from the blow, and left him no alternative but to work frenetically, concentrating effort on things that would provide guaranteed returns: broadcasting, book reviews, short stories and the weekly newspaper column. He temporarily abandoned the lifetime ambition to become a distinguished novelist.

> 'My productivity is based upon the spur of necessity. Perhaps there is something to be said for the Collector of Taxes after all! They are an experimental test of my thought processes instead of relying upon the fairly narrow perspective of personal observation

> and experience, which has no doubt caused me to be stereotyped as a "regional writer". I eventually want to prove that I can make a positive and original contribution to literature.' (16)

He could not escape the fact that he was at his best as a rural chronicler, or continue to ignore the friends who urged him to concentrate on those strengths. The critics had not been kind to the book that followed the successful trilogy: *Dance & Skylark,* an obscure title adopted from nautical slang for leisure periods, was written to coincide with the 1951 Festival of Britain. It revolved around a small town's modest emulation of the national event and would no doubt have attracted better reviews if he had restricted himself to rustic simplicity rather than allowing his imagination to run riot. Moore had sought to reflect a mood of optimism emerging from the festival of celebration as a contrast to the weariness and pessimism afflicting post-war England, but he over-elaborated the message and exaggerated his characters.

Midsummer Meadow followed and he was the first to admit that it was a disaster. The book attempted to exorcise too many personal demons in what should have been a simple countrified tale of a philanthropic landowner's attempt to save a site of botanical interest. It instead developed into a rant against authority and made little impact upon either critic or readers. The only favourable comment came from Orville Prescott, influential principal book critic for *The New York Times,* who thought Moore's prose 'chimed like a distant church bell on an August morn.' A collection of short stories entitled *Tiger, Tiger* appeared in the same year. H.E.Bates wrote words of encouragement – he said the stories, written with a light touch, had given him pleasure. Others did not agree: a dark psychological undercurrent pervaded many pages and the plots were inadequately woven to excite anticipation. A *Daily Telegraph* reviewer joined Moore's advisers by suggesting he refrain from the esoteric and permit his pen to flow where his roots lay. Circumstances forced him finally to heed the overwhelming and continuous advice received over several years and during the following decade, which was also to be his last, he wrote his most impressive body of work. None reached the commercial heights of the trilogy, but viewed collectively, the books served to support an estimation that he was his generation's most highly regarded countryside writer.

White Sparrow combined his talents as storyteller and naturalist; a tale set in rural England controversially dealt with elements of racial prejudice long before the subject became of significant public and political concern.

> 'The white house sparrow which spent last spring and summer with us has returned to our orchard. An albino's expectation of life in the wild state is necessarily brief as it has no natural camouflage.' (17)

Moore drew an analogy between the fate of an outcast bird and treatment meted out by a white community to a youth of mixed race: the story ranges over all human emotion and contains many vignettes from the author's personal observations of a similar situation in his own village. A.D.Peters sold the idea to Collins, but increasingly questioned the underlying theme and the treatment Moore gave it. On receiving the draft he admitted that it was beautifully written, although more a short story, and requiring a further hundred pages to pursue the fate of the two main characters before it could be regarded as a novel. He could not anticipate reviewers recommending it to readers if the ending, as suggested, left them in suspense. He thought the sensitivity of the material deserved further explanation to give substance to a tragedy embracing racial intolerance.

The author baulked at the criticism of his style and creative integrity, but more importantly, he could not brook undue delay, because he was desperately short of money.

> 'You are quite right to say that the story is without sub-plots – it is meant to be. I have apparently failed to get over to you that it ends naturally. Whatever happens subsequently to my two lovers is no part of the story. They will go their separate ways and another 100 pages on their fate would be an irrelevance.
>
> 'I conclude that you have not submitted the book to Collins; I conclude also that you assume he would be unwilling to pay the usual £500 advance. That provokes another financial crisis. Five months work, resulting in an unacceptable book, is a serious matter for any writer; in my case, it is catastrophic.
>
> 'The failure of *Midsummer Meadow* upset my budget. I reckoned the advance on *White Sparrow* would pay off the bank, building society arrears and enough of the income tax to keep the wolves from the door.' (18)

They eventually agreed a compromise: Moore refused to change the tone of his tale, but wrote another 9,000 words. Much to Peter's astonishment, William Collins thought it was the best thing his author had ever written, describing it as an idyllic tale of adolescent love; redolent with the scent of soft country air rising from its pages; conjuring the beauty of England as Shakespeare saw it and breaking new ground across barriers of convention! *White Sparrow* did well enough to alleviate the financial crisis, but although successfully adapted for radio, did not become a best-seller. In the same year John Moore published *The Season of the Year,* the first of his self-styled 'country contentments'. Writing about the natural world in a fervent poetic style, he devoted a chapter to each calendar month, confirming that often-expressed opinion of his admirers that he was at his best when concentrating on familiar territory. The next book would further prove the point.

'With the wolves temporarily at bay I got down to writing a long novel. It was a two-year job. We sold a lot of copies and suddenly the Big Dipper went up again.' (19)

September Moon was the product of a late-night conversation in the Savile about the romanticism of traditional Herefordshire hop harvests. Grand ideas for a film floated in alcoholic ether: John Moore was proposed as scriptwriter and he welcomed the opportunity to revisit one of his favourite areas and meet old friends. He wrote to several prominent Herefordshire growers and the replies convinced him that he would have more success with a book than the unfamiliar medium of film.

> 'We start picking in September – do come and explore. We have gypsies and people from Wales and the Black Country (Incidentally, the former prefer to be called travellers). Once they are sure you have nothing to do with rations, drains or income tax, I think you may find quite interesting material.' (20)

> 'My pickers are Welsh, with a vocabulary more suited to silent films! It will give me great pleasure to introduce you to one; Aunty Glad will probably say a great deal more than you require.' (21)

> 'If you could only write a book on hop growing and picking on the same lines as your others it would be just as good.' (22)

> 'Your average hop farm will cost £25,000; brewers usually outbid everyone and grab all that come on the market.
>
> 'Hops are ploughed down in March – the soil ploughed from either side of the plant or hill. Then the remaining soil is knocked away with a kerf and the root cut, or "thrown down", to the ground. The plants shoot in April and long shoots known as gut-wires are pulled off as they grow too much bine. We select and tie three shoots per string in May. Hop tying, or twiddling, are old terms, although the

> shoots are not tied, but twisted round the string in a clockwise direction. Then the roots are moulded to prevent further growth.' [23]

He accepted an invitation to savour the atmosphere at first-hand from John Hawkins, whose Thinghill Court Farm was a showcase for the industry. Lodging at the village pub, he spent two weeks among the pickers, and in the course of listening to raucous tales and witnessing their squabbles, made a lasting impression on John Hawkins' wife, Molly: 'He was a remarkable chap, spending a lot of time with the gypsies; drinking and dancing with them, and planting kisses on the women.'

> 'What fascinated me was the turbulence, the wildness, the Dionysian or Bacchanalian atmosphere of the month of September when the hops are picked. I thought I'd like to set a love story against this background of farmers, gypsies and the jungle-green hop-yards. It is a tale of something that is nearly done with, because, within the next two or three years, machines will replace the pickers. Hop picking is a roughish time and to that extent, the novel is roughish too: I wanted to put in the whole shooting match and the picture would have been incomplete if I had left out the more boisterous aspects.
>
> 'Those who say gypsies are more dirty and dishonest than the average tramp know as much about gypsies and tramps as a gamekeeper knows about vermin. (That is to say, he knows how to catch them sometimes and lay mischief at their door). Tramps and gypsies are the victims of perpetual guerrilla warfare waged against them by authority – constantly suspected, chivvied and chased for no better reason than that they have no use for our snug hearth-stones. I know more about them. I have found they are honest and a great deal cleaner in their habits than many

> slum-dwellers who have a roof over their heads. They have great courtesy, splendid independence and a sort of arrogance. Moreover, their children are not half as horrid as children who go to school.
>
> 'You watch them. The caravans with dogs under the axles, the crate of fowl slung at the back, the sly, strangely beautiful faces of the children peeping through the windows, the women who walk so proudly and yet so furtively, the babies slung in shawls: an alien people, a folk apart, whom we mistrust because they can't adapt themselves to our ways.
>
> 'And tramps are so respectable – milestone inspectors and cigarette-end collectors. They are always loners, taking the same annual route, being ruled by habit. Among the most law abiding of mortals, they may be dirty, but are largely honest. They hear all, see all and say nothing – having found freedom and discovered that it is only a word.' (24)

Those observations were not new: he always argued against those who sought to interfere with Romany independence. Barbara Cartland, another supporter of the gypsies, but with more altruistic motives, received short shrift for ideas of permanent sites to allow schooling for the children.

> 'It sounds to me like putting animals in cages and the gypsies will not put up with it. The caretaker would always be bullying them about hygiene, which they would not like. In any event, I do not want to educate their children in our way, or make them fit into our way of life. I think the gypsies should be allowed to live their own lives without being converted, cosseted, badgered or persuaded differently.' (25)

Moore could not know that within a few years traditional gypsy life would all but disappear, or that *September Moon* would immortalise their traditional world for all time in a rollicking tale of interaction between a stable farming community and its itinerant rough-and-ready workforce. A.D.Peters and Collins predicted a huge success, advertising the book widely and launching it in London bookshops festooned with hop bines.

Reviewers were not so enthusiastic, finding it lacked Moore's breezy charm and wit. Some accused him of unoriginality and repetitive themes from his previous novels, while others objected to a transfer of farmyard morals to a respectable farmhouse. He dismissed his detractors, saying that there was nothing in the book that would bring a blush to the face of a Victorian aunt. He was, nevertheless, devastated by criticism of what he regarded a more than satisfactory tale, and noted in his journal that it was the first time that he had been really savaged by the critics. He never forgave them.

Richard Church, a long-time admirer, leapt to his defence with a considered perspective:

> 'It captures so fully the atmosphere, the sensuous ripeness, which the author always imparts into his work. Not since Richard Jefferies died, have we had a spokesman of the English country life, the very spirit of place, who can conjure the smells, sights and sounds as well as the mysteries, silences and portents of night and day down on the farm, along the winding lanes, and through the lush woodland as John Moore does. In every detail of the habits and even the aberrations of the hop-pickers, Mr Moore is accurate in his portraiture. And in this fidelity, he has contrived to introduce two highly dramatic stories, of love and feud, to which many fiction critics have taken exception. I see nothing wrong in telling a good story and bringing it to a climax that makes the reader gasp for breath.' (26)

A complimentary review in *The Bookseller* also helped and sales eventually reached half-a-million. The Rank Organisation paid £6,000 for the film rights: Moore was again in funds and, driving a new Jaguar, took an extended holiday in France at the home of Monty Mackenzie. He also renewed his acquaintance with Gibraltar and southern Spain, while Lucile journeyed to visit her family in Australia for the first time since leaving for Europe in 1938.

Sadly, during their absence Ina Moore died after a short illness in January 1958, and John hurried home. He was alone and inconsolable: the one towards whom he always turned in times of difficulty was no longer there and his loss was shared by many who respected the old lady's selfless commitment and compassion to those she regarded as less fortunate than herself. At her funeral service at the Abbey, he quoted Chaucer: 'She used gladly to do well – Such was her manner every day.' Ina's death may have been the trigger for a steady decline in John's already delicate health: bouts of depression, glandular fever and stomach disorders became recurrent features of his existence.

Chapter 7

The Final Years – 1958-67

'I like arguing about things, especially politics, and in politics especially foreign affairs. But I wouldn't like to be a politician.' (1)

There were, however, more fundamental reasons for John Moore's delicate health than grieving for his mother: stress associated with his early years as a writer; wartime injuries and a weakened heart, and frustration created by an inability to repeat the huge successes of *Portrait of Elmbury* and *Brensham Village* all played a part. His volatile nature did not help matters: entrenched views about social injustice and a passionate defence of the rural environment constantly brought him into conflict with authority. He did not have his father's diffident and conciliatory manner; instead, he inherited the patrician nature of his mother's side of the family. Although companionable, kind and charming when it suited, he could never resist a challenge and was a force to be reckoned with when things were not to his liking.

Moore thrived on vigorous argument and did not gladly suffer fools. He was a committed member of the Labour Party from his early working days until becoming disillusioned with the post-war socialist government. After resigning, he canvassed opinions in conversation with a wide circle of acquaintances, maintaining a particular political discourse with Colin Jackson, Tewkesbury-born barrister, foreign affairs correspondent and fervent socialist with aspirations to become a Member of Parliament.

> 'I wish I could be a Liberal so that my vote could demonstrate my dislike for the other two parties, my

contempt for their record and my dismay at their politics.

'Before the war I always voted Labour. I had witnessed mass unemployment, shocking poverty and social injustice everywhere. Also the Tories appeased dictators. I campaigned and voted for Labour and am proud of it.

'I now have no sympathy for union attitudes or hag-ridden Labour politics; the intellectuals are so anti-British. There is too much bureaucracy, but neither do I have sympathy with big business. So what will influence my vote? Foreign policy. Liberal policy, so far as it exists, demands that we abandon the bomb while continuing to shelter under the umbrella of the Yanks. That seems cowardly and quite out of accord with what I want my country's attitude to be … I will vote Tory.

'It was very agreeable to see you on Sunday, though I'm afraid I gave you a rather rough reception. The tender-hearted Lucile thought I was a bit unmannerly. I would never wish to be that with you dear chap. Now about the nice mess the American Secretary of State is getting us in.' (2)

Jackson described their heated discussions as akin to lectures by a Professor Moore in the style of a pompous *Daily Telegraph* editorial, but nothing pleased his adversary more than news of his selection to contest a safe Labour seat.

'I once delivered a lecture in your constituency. It was a day of murk and fog. I drove through a conurbation, which I did not believe could exist outside the industrial suburbs of hell itself. I hope there will be plenty of people to vote for you and to get you into Parliament – as a livener-up of what I still consider to be a lost cause.' (3)

Jackson became an MP and some years later Moore announced his intention of returning to the socialist fold. He became exercised by the Southern Rhodesia question because of discussions with his cousin Sir Jack Corbett, a successful tobacco farmer and member of the Rhodesian legislature. Corbett wished to meet Prime Minister Harold Wilson during a London visit to press for military intervention in opposition to Ian Smith's declaration of unilateral independence. Moore shamelessly used the promise of reversion to socialism in return for Jackson's intervention:

> 'If there is an election this Spring I shall vote for your lot.' (4)

Unfortunately, Jackson did not know that Wilson regarded Corbett as a spent force in Rhodesian politics and was peremptorily told to mind his own business. It was some little time before he and Moore were reconciled.

Moore engaged in many disputes with authority just for the hell of it: taking local politicians to task, questioning chief constables about police practices, and hounding humbug and hypocrisy wherever they arose.

> 'On the night of 23 December my secretary was driving home and was stopped by two policemen, who said they were doing a check to try to catch criminals. They asked her where she had come from and where she was going. It happens that she is the second girl I know who has been stopped in similar circumstances. It occurs to me that there are dangers in this practice. What business of the police is it to enquire where they had been and to where they were going. I am afraid that I should flatly refuse to answer. Every good citizen wants to help the police, but it is desperately important to preserve our precious freedoms and rise in defence of the least suggestion of a police state.

Police interrogation into innocent people's private affairs is intolerable.' (5)

'The Tewkesbury magistrates last week refused to grant an extension of licensing hours during the period of the annual Mop Fair. The chairman said they did so with sorrow because the application by licensees had been granted for many years. Your Police Inspector had objected on the grounds that the fair was not a special occasion and said he was acting on instructions. Presumably, the instructions were yours. Perhaps you would be good enough to publicly explain to the good citizens of this town how you reach the conclusion that their annual celebration, which has taken place for hundreds of years, is nothing special, and, furthermore, why you have suddenly decided to curtail their enjoyment of it?' (6)

'Two girls, aged 21 and 22 booked into a hotel with American servicemen, signing their real names, but with the prefix "Mrs". They were charged under the Aliens Order of 1920 and sentenced to one month's imprisonment. Another girl who had stayed at a boarding house alone, but under an assumed name, was given an absolute discharge. I am very disturbed at the disparity, which smacks of discrimination on moral, rather than criminal grounds. Police and magistrates are not censors of morals and I regard the former case as a repugnant use of the law against British subjects.' (7)

'There has been a rash of prosecutions for publishing obscene material. Before we fall further into such foolishness would it not be wise to return to the *modus vivendi* – a typically English compromise which has existed for the past twenty years and which worked admirably until the present "purity" campaign erupted. In other words, let the police, who really know very little about literature, get on with the job for which they are qualified and intended; and let serious novelists get on with theirs.' (8)

Anyone who crossed him ran the risk of retribution and he had a long memory. In 1945, Canon Brian Purefoy, who succeeded Edward Gough as vicar of Tewkesbury during the war years, distressed Lucile by examining her religious beliefs during a visit to her sickbed. Moore reacted furiously:

'My wife has her own views on religion. They are different to mine – I am not a Christian – but they are her business. The sick room is not a place for such discussions and you took unfair advantage. My mother is a devoted member of your congregation – come as her friend, not as an argumentative priest – or not at all until my wife is better.' (9)

That outwardly minor slight created a rift between the two men and exaggerated another issue that became widely referred to as 'The Second Battle of Tewkesbury'. After the war, Moore rejoined the Abbey Friends as a council member, and had been surprised to discover that the capital fund amounted to only £1,735, with little evidence of expenditure on structural refurbishment. Purefoy, left largely to his own devices during the war years, had used a major part on pet projects for which it was not intended – namely the refurbishment of organs and fabric. When the full council reconvened the vicar asked for a further £700, giving Moore an ideal opportunity to avenge Lucile's distress:

'We are skint. We have no leeway for another 'loan' to the organ fund. We have squandered the whole of our funds on the damned organs. Despite Purefoy's admirable projects, to me it seems imperative that we should keep capital intact against a catastrophe which old buildings are subject to from time to time.' (10)

The vicar, denied his money, somewhat ungraciously entered into a dispute, bringing unwanted publicity and embarrassment to the council. He set about undermining its authority, declaring one prominent member involved in divorce proceedings as unsuitable for office, scurrying among his congregation to solicit support and, finally, threatening resignation unless The Friends' secular constitution changed to preclude anyone who was not a practising member of the Church of England. It was unclear who won the battle of wills.

> 'The constitution cannot be changed except by democratic means. The vicar's attitude is hypocritical, because we know there are many occasions when he has administered to and associated with divorcees and other sinners – there are enough of both within his congregation. His proposals would exclude the many Jews, Catholics, Nonconformists, atheists and agnostics who wish to preserve the Abbey and contribute to our funds.
>
> 'The vicar is a plain ass. I could not continue to be a Friend if we are to institute a sort of vicar's Gestapo to inquire into the private lives of our councillors.
>
> 'The Friends have had an unhappy history during these post-war years. I would have no contribution to make if I were to stay.' (11)

Moore resigned and totally ignored the vicar throughout the remainder of his ministry. It was not until Purefoy's retirement that he volunteered to help once again in raising another £25,000 for Abbey repairs. He was, however, never reconciled with the Established Church and continued to create many a stir with personal observations about the Christian faith

In an article entitled *Why Should Christians be so Miserable* he explained the reasons for his loss of belief. He was never, he wrote, able to reconcile the piety and solemnity of religious celebration with a God who supposedly created a world of beauty, excitement and optimism. Considerably influenced at an early age by his father's death, he particularly grew to question the negative incantation of universal sin implied in the words of the burial service: *have mercy upon us miserable sinners – man that is born of woman has but a short time to live and is full of misery – deliver this our brother out of this sinful world.* However, it was not until inducted as a full member of the church at a particularly sanctimonious confirmation service that he finally rejected religion as being so much hypocrisy. 'My agnosticism stems from the fact that I am quite incapable of believing in a God who prefers sad faces to cheerful ones, gravity to laughter, misery to joy, death to life.'

Of course, such views were distressing for his pious mother; she could not understand her son's sensitive appreciation of all Creation while dismissing The Maker. It is unfortunate that she did not live to read the words of Leonard Birch following John's death only nine years after her own. The Rector of Bredon, who often supped with him in The Fox and Hounds, put the dichotomy into context:

> 'I always called him my favourite agnostic. He would be amused that I should write a gratuitous appreciation of him. He lampooned the clergy and criticised the Establishment whether it was ecclesiastical, political or social, because he was a man of complete integrity and intellectual honesty, and abominated humbug in any form. He had immense reverence for life and a love of beauty, and his rejection of the Christian religion was intellectual rather than a personal dislike of the ministry.
>
> 'He could not square in his mind, I think, the concept of a God of love with the problems of evil, pain

> and suffering. Though he was almost militantly agnostic, he was, however, no atheist. His God was one of Beauty and Order, and the Creator of lovely things. Here for him was Truth, and in the world of flowers and birds, of horses, and fish and living creatures, he approached and knew God.
>
> 'I stood in his lovely garden, feeling the spirit of the man and thought of the words: "Whatsoever things are true, whatsoever things are honourable, whatsoever things are just, whatsoever things are pure, whatsoever things are lovely, whatsoever things are of good report, think on these things." He often did, and his world was bounded by them. He was able, through the nobility of his mind and mastery of words, to communicate the magic of these things to others.' (12)

In a completely different milieu, as member and sometime Chairman of the Society of Authors, Moore was able to use his contrary nature and strength of character to good effect. He was by no means the only author to suffer from the burden of higher rates of personal taxation that consistently refused to make allowances for the precarious nature of the profession. His friend T.H.White (Tim), author of *The Once and Future King* and a tax exile in Alderney, who made a fortune from the adaptation of his book into the hit musical Camelot, was particularly embittered. He dubbed post-war Britain 'The Farewell State'; complaining that, after taxation, he had only received ten per cent of a $28,000 prize from the American Book of the Month Club, and anticipated that he would only benefit from a quarter of his total American earnings for any year. Tongue-in-cheek, he asked if the hero of John Moore's next novel could shoot the Chancellor of the Exchequer as an act of public service! H.E.Bates, another hard-working, successful, yet frustrated author, resigned from what he considered an impotent society incapable of negotiating with the Inland Revenue on behalf of its members. Having served his country in the RAF throughout the Second World War and thereafter struggling to educate his children, he equated literary achievement with the kiss of death. Several more well-known names threatened to break away and create a more militant Writers' Union, among them Compton Mackenzie, Eric Linklater, Osbert Sitwell and A.P.Herbert.

Moore was arrogant enough not to be cowed by this *illuminati* and, to his great credit, held the Society together. With steely determination he secured a change in fiscal policy by reasoning that the Chancellor of the Exchequer, R.A.Butler, himself an author, would be open to a logical argument from a delegation. After a splendid Savoy lunch, Butler paved the way for a meeting with Inland Revenue policy makers, eventually leading to an arrangement for extension of assessment of time restrictions to ease the burden of fluctuating royalties. It was a considerable coup and elevated Moore's standing in the eyes of more influential contemporaries.

'My Family have lived here for well over three hundred years and I could not contemplate living elsewhere. Mind you, that does not mean that everything about it is perfect, but there is much that is worth retaining and only fools would contemplate wholesale change.' (13)

Moore's last campaign concerned events closer to home. He had great affection for his native town, was steeped in its history and yeoman culture and determined that its heritage be preserved from wanton modernisation and development. He was not against projects sympathetic to the unique environs, but viewed many proposals with suspicion, convinced that they had more to do with convenience and commercial greed than actual necessity. He favoured renovation of old buildings rather than replacement and thought that any unavoidable development should be sympathetic to existing architectural and natural vistas. He therefore found himself incapable of remaining silent when town planners proposed large-scale demolition to accommodate contemporary featureless structures.

Demands for change had gathered momentum over several years. Ever-increasing motorised traffic caused untold damage to ancient buildings and made life intolerable for residents and shoppers alike. There had been little investment in housing or industry after the Second World War; many slums remained and people left the town in search of better conditions. John Moore had foreseen the problems in his contentious 1931 articles and returned to the theme three decades later by attacking the same familiar targets.

In the early Sixties there was talk of the town becoming a designated housing and industrial overspill development area for the West Midlands conurbation. The *Tewkesbury Register* leaked proposals to release enough agricultural land to provide thousands of houses and create sufficient employment for the inhabitants. Another suggestion was the development of the rivers to offer a nationwide leisure facility accessed from new junctions on the M5 motorway and thereby increasing existing road usage by a factor of ten.

> 'We risk destroying the town we know and love. Why this passion for bigness? To whose advantage is it to make Tewkesbury an overspill area or a BIG industrial town? Why triple the population? Will it be a better place in which to live? No! The only gain will be to big business, self-important town councillors and bureaucrats anxious to extend their influence.' (14)

Moore stood accused of wishing to retain the slums and obstructing the Town Council's attempts to grow under its own terms before being dragooned into change by a larger dictatorial local authority.

> 'To Hell with our borough status, mayor and town crier, if by doing so we can retain the historic nature of this town. It has been vandalised over more than thirty years by piecemeal, disastrous and ludicrous

> developments. I am accused of wanting to keep the slums – nothing could be further from the truth – I have campaigned against them since the Twenties and described their horror in books. I do plead guilty to criticising an utterly unimaginative housing development on a prime southerly facing site overlooking the town and thank my stars that the flood plain will prevent its expansion.' (15)

He was not without support: some of it coming from unexpected quarters. The local press published a letter from a New Zealand visitor, Jenny Day:

> 'Tewkesbury is dirty, shabby and running down gently. What used to be a beautiful town filled with historical interest is rapidly becoming a wilderness of derelict buildings. No visitor can bear the thunder of continuous heavy traffic, nor wish to gaze on once lovely buildings, now dirty and abandoned. Can nothing be done, before it is too late for Tewkesbury?' (16)

Furthermore, her comments and those of a number of Americans stimulated an article illustrated by photographs of tumbledown buildings in the *Daily Telegraph* which touched raw nerves. Town Clerk, Kenneth Smales, was quick to defend his employers by diverting responsibility towards national government policy, but could do nothing to avoid a generally held belief that the Council was incapable of finalising any original thought or coherent policy. Smales personally favoured wholesale modern development and infuriated Moore by publicly labelling their disagreements as an issue between Progressives and Medievalists. The Abbey Lawn Cottages, he said, proved the point: the derelict fifteenth-century tradesmen's houses adjacent to The Abbey were continuing to deteriorate and no one was prepared to decide their future.

> 'The Americans think the Town Clerk is walking the streets with a sledgehammer, knocking down all the buildings he comes across. Discussions about Abbey Lawn cottages have been going on for twenty years. At this rate, we shall be talking about the same properties in a hundred years. Unless there is some concrete suggestion forthcoming there is a proposal that these buildings will be included in a clearance area.' (17)

'A Battle between Meds and Progs', repeated the *Daily Mail* when John Moore came to the defence of those ancient buildings. Constant dithering over what he considered the jewels in the crown of the town's domestic architecture exasperated him.

> 'I am described as a Med. I never mind what I am called. I accept change, but mankind has it in his power to control and direct it. I want it to proceed orderly and yet imaginatively, not by way of a greedy scramble for profit and prestige. I want for my native town a future as splendid as its past; for we shall be a grovelling generation indeed if we build meanly and selfishly within a mile of Tewkesbury's Abbey tower. We should look upon the town as a cherished heritage, conserving the beauty that has been handed down to us. Progress is not necessarily served by the destruction of what is beautiful or what is old, nor necessarily equated with the profit of speculators, the prestige of officials, or the pomposity of councillors.
>
> 'The development of our town is tortuous; there is no steady aim or object.' (18)

The public nature of the debate stirred consciences and forced a public enquiry. The Council delayed the issue of compulsory purchase notices for privately owned property, but did not defer the demolition of some in public ownership. Moore was determined to prevent further destruction and lobbied his

Member of Parliament, Nicholas Ridley, and the Minister for Local Government. He played his trump card, however, by securing the support of an old and influential friend.

John Betjeman happened to be researching a series of BBC documentaries about England's architectural heritage and agreed to include Tewkesbury among the places he visited. The Town Council postponed wholesale demolitions when John Moore let slip that he was supplying Betjeman's research material.

> 'Tewkesbury has one hundred timber framed buildings dating from the 16th and 17th centuries in the three main streets, many showing the signs of the conversions that the owners carried out over the years to bring them into line with fashions of the day. On the upper stories of the finest examples can be seen the jetty, or overhang, each extending out over the floor below to offer it protection from the elements.
>
> 'A characteristic of the town is its alleyways; originally providing access to open land and storage areas behind premises fronting the main streets, the gaps were later utilised to provide living accommodation and workshops, and eventually, many of them degenerated into the notorious slums. They were a utilisation of precious space in a place prone to flood waters.
>
> 'There is one central feature that looms over all, and around which the whole place seems to be built. This is the Abbey with its enormous square tower – the finest Norman tower in the world! Its weathered stone takes the light from the sky and seems to change as the weather changes – grey as a ghost on misty days – pale primrose in the bright sun – old rose in the evening – and in the light of a red sunset, it burns with a sort of inward light, as if it were afire.
>
> 'Then there are the timber framed cottages close by the Abbey, built originally as shop premises to

serve its monastery; twenty-three in all, although only seventeen survive. They are narrow in construction, just over eleven feet wide, with frontages onto the street and rear walls abutting the original monastery wall. The window shutter of the front room was designed to lower horizontally onto the street, to form a counter upon which the occupiers displayed their wares. The only other rooms are a small scullery at the rear and a first floor bedroom.' (19)

Betjeman's programme could do nothing for buildings already razed, but did ensure the preservation of the Abbey cottages. Had he lived, Moore would be pleased to see the row now restored to its former glory and one of the cottages housing the countryside museum in his name. A number of preservation orders saved many other notable structures from rapacious wholesale development. While there still exist some who comment adversely about the rape of Tewkesbury's original commercial centre, the continuing neglect of some old structures and the aesthetic quality of modern developments, it remains a fact that the campaign spearheaded by Moore saved many of the town's unique characteristics.

'For several years, rather than grind away in pursuit of money or fame, I wrote about things that took my fancy, enjoyed myself as a naturalist and fished a lot of water with like-minded companions.' (20)

The publication of *September Moon* and regular income from broadcasting, and newspaper and magazine articles enabled John Moore to adopt a more relaxed lifestyle as he tried to regain his health. He devoted more time to leisure activities, building up his collection of bugs and moths from local woodland, shooting over water meadows beside the Avon and again fishing the best sporting water in Britain and Ireland. His output of full-length books was restricted to a novel – *Jungle Girl* – and two volumes of country essays: *Man, Bird & Beast* and *Come Rain, Come Shine*. The essays he wrote for the self-styled 'country contentments' distilled into words for everyone's enjoyment the very essence of hedgerows, hayfields, village greens, rivers and streams.

Jungle Girl was different, an example of Moore's restless creativity and desire to rediscover the popularity achieved by his most successful books. In it, he lengthened a previously successful short story about a teenage fairground snake charmer into a novelette and sent the draft for comment to the master of the genre, H.E.Bates. Bates commended the quality of what he described as a lively, touching and endearing story, written in Moore's recognisable meandering, semi-colloquial style. The assessment no doubt pleased Moore and may have helped convince a sceptical A.D.Peters about the book's worth. Peters was only persuaded to take it to Collins on receipt of Bates' opinion, but his original doubts were confirmed when publication met with poor reviews and disappointing sales.

Moore's reaction to another failure was to take a break, indulging himself in a period of reflection from which emerged a surprisingly popular book.

> 'Word books long ago quickened my interest and sharpened my curiosity about these tools of my trade. I will write a different kind of word book; one that reflects the fun, excitement, wonder and sense of exploration among the minds of man, which I have found in my dealings with words as a writer and reader.' (21)

He intended it as a form of academic therapy and wrote leisurely, weaving a raft of stories around English usage. Both Peters and William Collins were enthusiastic about the draft he produced; their only reservation concerned its title. 'A Lover of Words', suggested Peters, while Collins favoured 'A Trove of Words'. However, Moore, for his own good reasons, insisted upon *You English Words* – it was the first line of Edward Thomas's poem 'Words', and it had remained in his memory since writing the earlier biography.

> 'You English Words/I know you/You are light as dreams/Tough as oak/Precious as gold/As poppies and corn/or an old cloak.' (22)

Within a few months of publication twenty-three thousand copies had sold at home and in the American market, with Collins confidently printing a further ten thousand. C.S.Forester, to whom the book was dedicated, reviewed it enthusiastically; and Eric Partridge, the veteran lexicographer and author of several philological studies, commented that Moore regarded all words in the manner of Shakespeare, with the shrewdness of a master-craftsman, the eye of an artist and the curiosity of a historian. *You English Words,* he said, was written by a man who used words as the tools of his craft, with a respect and appreciation of their power and beauty.

Collins ordered another substantial reprint when *The Times Education Supplement* recommended the book as having the potential to create a divine discontent in anyone previously satisfied with a basic vocabulary. The only dissenting voices came from members of the Esperanto Society offended by some unnecessarily flippant remarks.

> 'Esperanto seems to have a curious effect upon the people who go to the trouble of learning it.
>
> 'They soon begin to regard it not so much a language as a cause. It makes a lot of people happy, and I can do no more than confess my humble opinion that these people are rather odd. I cannot see any point or purpose whatever in an artificial language.' (23)

The paragraph inspired an orchestrated campaign of abuse that goaded Moore into further provocation.

> 'I think all artificial languages are rather silly. I don't withdraw a word. I think the whole concept of Esperanto is a little absurd, and of course, I shall

> continue to say so. Esperantists are very fierce indeed. I don't think I know any people as fierce unless they are vegetarians, and very often Esperantists are vegetarians as well. It is really like a wasps' nest: if you disturb one the whole lot start buzzing at you.' (24)

The storm in a teacup soon subsided.

You English Words earned enough money for John and Lucile to begin the realisation of a dream to own a house with sufficient land to keep horses and create natural habitats for wild birds and small mammals. They chose Lower Mill Farm with its views over open countryside; solidly built of Bredon stone it stood beside the Squitter Brook, at the end of a secluded lane in lower Kemerton. It retained its original character with a massive waterwheel and millpond, but needed extensive restoration.

> 'Farmers don't bother with gardens. At The Mill, there were no flowerbeds; the only concession to horticulture was that the small rough field at the front was described as a lawn. There was a rough track across it, which was called a drive and to my great joy, there was running water everywhere. The Squitter Brook meandered through the orchard, broadened into swamp of what was once the millpond, before spilling onto the motionless black wheel. It then ran beneath the house and on its way through the paddocks towards the river.' (25)

It was an ideal setting for a naturalist, enabling Moore to observe wildlife from his study, stock the stream running beneath its window with trout and plant areas of pasture with flora to attract butterflies and insects. The acquisition of a horse added to his contentment and for the first time in his life he appeared secure and at peace with himself:

> 'I bought myself a thoroughbred bay mare, called Zena: quick and tireless and sensitive and gay. From her back I watched the seasons come and go.' (26)

He became besotted with his frivolously temperamental companion, about whom readers of *Country Column* were regularly informed.

> 'Zena was terribly naughty. For most of the time, she was up on end at horrible angles. Then a pheasant got up under her feet, I sped for miles through the air and rolled over three times, quite unhurt though winded ... Her stable companion is a domestic fowl desperate for company called Henny. She has taken up residence – and there spends most of her days. She pecks up the oats which Zena spills, scratches in the straw among Zena's feet, and is never in danger of being kicked or trampled. While Zena munches hay, Henny perches on the edge of her manger: and while Zena puts her head over the loose-box half-door Henny flies up and sits there, a few inches from her nose.
>
> 'One of the cats, Sammy, gets on well with Zena. They touch noses in an affectionate way and Sammy purrs. It is extraordinary how easy he seems to be with this huge creature. But not all the cats like Zena; nor does she like any other than Sammy.' (27)

Their rides together over Bredon Hill were originally intended as leisurely relaxation, but he could not break the habit of recording daily observations and his journal soon contained sufficient material for another 'country contentment' – *The Year of the Pigeons.*

> 'The back of a horse is the best vantage point from which to view the country and all about me lay the land which I love best in all England. I rode Zena far a-

> field, up and over our hill, with its oak woods and spring pastures, through the market gardens where a score of assorted crops makes a many coloured hem all around the green skirts of the hill; down the deep lanes, between flowering hedgerows; along the banks of our stream where the mills have clanked since Doomsday; over the common, beside the slow river, or far across country to look at the haunts of my boyhood again.
>
> 'I got to know the familiar land in a way I had never known it before. I saw it changing before my eyes. The new motor road slashed through it, the suburbs crept out and out from the little towns, and immemorial elms came down, as did the cider apple trees, which no longer served any purpose but to delight the eye. I saw how the new techniques of scientific agriculture imposed their new totalitarian order upon the land.
>
> 'I would look across the county from Zena's back and see, spread out before me, a battlefield in which the tragic conflict between man and nature was being bitterly fought out.' [28]

The book, an almanac of the rustic year, inspired in the first instance by the unusually severe winter of 1963, is probably the most evocative of the series.

> 'One evening about a week after Christmas, we all became aware of "something coming". There was a distinct, but indefinable change in the quality of the cold. The difference between today's wind and yesterday's was like the difference between iron and steel. The cold strode across Gloucestershire and we heard the wind of its passing as we lay in bed. At first, there was nothing to be seen but the blurred grey-white of thick snow blown horizontally. We were snowed in and the wind howled louder and the snow froze hard.

> 'About a fortnight after the start of the great frost, the pigeons descended upon us like a plague. Vast flocks came with the bitter wind out of the north; descending from the snowy sky upon fields in which the sprout tops were the only green things to be seen against the blanket of white. This invasion was a large scale war, conducted on one side with a recklessness of desperation, on the other with the ruthlessness and brutality of men defending their very livelihood against creatures so pitifully crazed by hunger that they forgot all fear, defying the guns to come in head-high onto the sprouts.
>
> 'A flock of a thousand pigeons would light upon a fifteen acre field and leave nothing edible for man or bird.' [29]

It was an immediate success and brought welcome royalties. Nevertheless, John fell into the same trap that had ruined his father – overstretching himself to create the property of his dreams – and he needed a deal more money to complete the project. The leisurely life of gentleman author and broadcaster came to an end and, once again, at the age of fifty-four, circumstances dictated that he take up his pen and work with the required discipline and effort finally to produce a book that would fulfil his ambition to become a reputable novelist.

'Ah, my friend, you have written a VERY good book. I enjoyed it from beginning to end: it is by far the best thing you have done.' [30]

Writing *The Waters Under the Earth* occupied him for four years, working conscientiously as his health allowed and hardly daring to believe that he would ever reach the end. Consequently, he told his journal more about it than either agent or publisher:

> 'It is by far the longest and most ambitious novel I have attempted. It is a story about the decline of a

> landowning family, whose fortune was founded in the days of the first Elizabeth, and the uprising of some of the new, brash, tough, adventurous children of the squire's gardener – about the going down of an old England and the rising up of a new.' (31)

His theme drew an analogy between the incomparable power of nature that he personally experienced when trying to control flooding at his home and that of the British post-war working class.

> 'The waters reached everywhere: runnels like the veins in a gorgonzola cheese, seeping, shaking, bubbling, ever questing and testing for an easier way to achieve the eternal ambition of all water to find its own level and at last to be still.' (32)

The social commentary, tracing a declining influence of the aristocracy, was one that Moore, former socialist, but scion of the liberal-conservative middle class, considered himself uniquely qualified to analyse.

The Seldon family lived at Doddington Manor for four hundred years, the time taken for the parkland oaks, which still provided shelter for the few remaining red squirrels in England to mature. In Moore's story, the established order is threatened. The squirrels fall to the predations of their grey cousins, the oaks follow to make way for a new road, and an invasion of wealthy and unsentimental industrialists threaten Sir Ferdo Seldon's tenure. In addition, the impoverished aristocrat must come to terms with an employee's subversive aspirations for social equality.

Seldon's solution is to isolate himself from a society that he has no wish to be part of and leave his only child to determine the fate of the crumbling estate. Susan Seldon, just home from finishing school and anticipating a genteel life before eventual marriage and children, is obliged rapidly to mature and accept responsibility both for her aging parents and the estate. It is an involved story of politics and romance, drawn together by a master draughtsman and told with rustic charm and social awareness.

> 'The book was finished in the New Year of 1965. My publisher was off to Australia on a business trip and desperately wanted to read it before he left; and I fell ill – quite ill – with only ten thousand words left to write. I lay abed and thought about my overdraft and how very absurd it would be if I pegged out with the book so nearly done: not worth a penny until the last sentence is written.
>
> 'Anyhow I recovered; the book was done. Billy Collins read it in three days and told me he was going to print more copies than he'd ever printed of anything of mine before.' (33)

A.D.Peters, who had thought that Moore's health would prevent him writing another full- length book, responded enthusiastically to the raw typescript. A number of respected literary figures asked to copy-edit echoed his own opinion that it was 'quintessentially Moore and a book Shakespeare would have enjoyed'. Compton Mackenzie said he read every word, regarding it as a masterpiece without fault and a depiction of character and landscape that would bring joy to the reading world. Richard Church expressed the view that the story would crown Moore's career with a huge success and particularly commended the spacious humanity and passion of the narrative. William Collins paid an unprecedented advance of £3,000, *Woman's Own* magazine bid £2,500 for the serialisation rights, forty-eight thousand copies sold within three months on the UK market and an additional twenty thousand in the United States placed it tenth on the American list of best sellers.

The reviews surpassed anything Moore had received since the publication of Portrait of Elmbury. His wartime colleague, Nicholas Monsarrat, described *The Waters Under the Earth* as a beautiful, haunting book that refreshed the post-war countryside to its former glory, encapsulating the developing aspirations of a burgeoning lower class. Orville Prescott, of *The New York Times,* had previously reviewed several of Moore's books and read *The Waters Under the Earth* while on a retirement holiday in Scotland. It was, he said in a letter to the author, the finest novel to pass through his hands in the previous five years, in fact, since Harper Lee's *To Kill a Mocking Bird.* He enthused about its natural beauty, wisdom, fictional skill and perceptive understanding of social change – praise indeed from someone who never hesitated to heap criticism on any writer who did not meet the highest standards.

Smith's Trade News predicted that the book would attract the vast readership enjoyed by writers such as Howard Spring, encouraging Peters to begin negotiating the translation and publishing rights in France, Denmark, Spain and Italy. John Moore had seemingly achieved the goal he set himself when leaving the auctioneer's office some thirty-five years previously and somewhat portentously wrote to Peters:

> 'In future will you persuade The Telegraph (or anybody else) not to describe me as "a writer on the countryside", but as a novelist. I think if a chap's novels sell twenty or thirty thousand he deserves to be described like that.' (34)

His euphoria was, however, short-lived due to the return of ill health. He was never again well enough to write intensively and the only other publication to appear under his name was a small volume of short stories for the American market entitled *Among the Quiet Folks.* He honoured his commitment to *Country Column* and continued to write short magazine articles, but his exclusive concern now was for Lucile's future welfare.

All immediate income from *The Waters Under the Earth* went to settle a bank overdraft and demands from the Inland Revenue. Although reasonably expecting the book to earn well, he pestered

Collins to reissue his more popular publications as added insurance: only three of the fifteen he had written since the war remained in print. However, the publisher was interested only in another original novel. Peters, encouraging him along the same lines, became heartened by suggestions in early 1967 that a romantic tale about medieval Cotswold shepherds and wool-traders was in the pipeline.

> 'When I was working on my new novel last night, I realised suddenly it was growing in scope and aims, and I saw I would need 150,000 to do justice to my story instead of 100,000. I dare not hurry it at this stage.
>
> 'Collins and Lippincotts [American publishers] should not expect the m/s until June or July. Financially we are OK for the next three years owing to the luck we have had with *The Waters* [*sic*] – the German book club deal and the American paperback.
>
> 'With an easier mind I will go steadily with this new novel and take a good holiday when I have finished it; round about mid summer, I hope.' (35)

In truth, all he did was to fiddle around with an idea for a four-volume anthology of natural history – one for each season of the year – comprising previously published articles and some new material. He completed the as yet unpublished Spring volume while distracted by a premonition that he had not long to live and the consequent preoccupation with personal matters.

He spent the first part of the year seeking the companionship of old friends: 'Pip' Foster, a fellow Territorial Army officer from the early days; Mike Daunt, the retired dashing test pilot and Edward Stephens – Ted of the schoolboy quartet from *Portrait of Elmbury*. It was Stephens, back in Tewkesbury after a career as a London surgeon, who persuaded him to consult his doctor when he began to show the obvious signs of serious illness.

John Moore was not eating properly, experienced difficulty in swallowing and lost weight rapidly. Dr Graham Shepherd, son of the former family GP, referred him to a consultant surgeon at Bristol's Frenchay Hospital, who discovered an advanced tumour in the oesophagus and recommended immediate surgery. After telling Lucile he wrote to his sister:

> 'It is easier to tell you this in a letter. I'm just back from hospital where they investigated my inside ... I have a tumour on the oesophagus and it will be operated on a week today ... the future is a bit uncertain.' (36)

He warned William Collins and his literary executors – A.D.Peters and Eric Linklater – before beginning to put his affairs in order. The most difficult letter was to his dearest friend – the octogenarian Sir Compton 'Monty' Mackenzie.

> 'I hate to write you a distressing letter, but such friends as you had better hear it straight from me and not from anyone else ... I think all will be well, but if things should go wrong will you ask Lucile to come out to you. Pradelles and you would do more for her than anything' (37)

Lucile was unable even to think about what the future might hold and spent the days before his admission to hospital in mental turmoil.

> 'On Saturday we had lunch at the Redesdale Arms at Moreton-in-Marsh. He wanted to go to the places we both enjoyed going to. While we were there, we looked at Warneford House, where his mother spent her life before marriage, and where his grandfather and great-grandfather were doctors. We pottered around Lower Mill on Sunday and Monday. John put a brave face on

> things, but we both found it impossible to talk about the following days.
>
> 'On Tuesday we were up very early. John said goodbye to Jeff and Sharleen, who saw us off. The garden with the begonias and petunias was looking beautiful. I was sure he would come back to it in two or three weeks, but I think he knew that there was only a remote chance.' (38)

Ten days later, his secretary Sharleen Pearce handed her an envelope. John had died and it contained his last letter.

> 'Beloved – I wrote you a letter like this before, when I was off to invade Normandy. I gave it to Anthony [Kimmins] to hand to you in the event that I did not make it, but all was well. Sharleen is going to look after this and you will only have it if I fail to survive. The odds are my condition does not give me a very long expectation anyway, but I want to live as long as I possibly can in order to be with you. You are the only one I have ever truly loved and today I love you more than ever. You have been and are the best wife any man could have, ever. You will grieve I know, but you must stop grieving one day and get down to making a new life for yourself. I am frightened of nothing save being without you.
>
> 'Be brave. One day someone may want to marry you. I shouldn't mind if he deserved you – Your Johnnie.' (39)

On 28 July, 1967 the *Birmingham Evening Mail* made the first public announcement:

> 'John Moore died last night. For eighteen years, he had brought country scenes and country life to readers in his weekly column. Today we print his last article, written while waiting to go into hospital.

> *"I think otter-hunting is a despicable pastime. I am equally opposed to badger digging, and the common seal is another mammal, which is becoming scarce in some parts, because of ruthless hunting for the sale of its skin."'* (40)

Moore proved himself a conservationist to the end. Within a few years, the legal protection afforded those three species and several other campaigns had eventually changed the face of the countryside. His efforts ensured the introduction of legislation to preserve ancient hedgerows, changed practices for the use of agricultural chemicals and increased awareness of the need to protect wildlife habitats.

Immediate family and a few close friends attended a simple committal at Cheltenham's crematorium. There was no memorial service and his ashes were interred without ceremony in the family plot beneath the walls of the ancient building he adored.

> 'John Moore did much for the Abbey, whenever there were appeals for its restoration; and to his affection for it his own writings bear testimony.' (41)

Sequel

'I am driven mad by my bloody Income Tax, trying to get the accounts right before they chop me.' (1)

John Moore adored Lucile and would have done anything to avoid burdening her with the problems his untimely death brought about. Unfortunately, he never took time efficiently to organise or manage his affairs, preferring to live from day-to-day and allowing the future to care for itself. Consequently, she endured several difficult years trying to hang on at Lower Mill Farm while lawyers and accountants settled the estate. In normal circumstances *The Waters Under the Earth,* widely regarded as a great novel, would have secured her future, but for some inexplicable reason sales fell away after John's death and the transcription rights were never finalised. The book, quickly forgotten, did not realise the predicted fortune.

Moore left a complex trail of tax credits and liabilities. Ownership in many of his copyright properties was uncertain: some he had sold in time of need, together with original manuscripts and it was difficult to ascertain exactly what Lucile would inherit. When all issues were resolved, she received little more than £10,000 and was unable to keep the house without further capital or substantial income. She tried commercially to exploit her former leisure interest in jewellery design, spent short periods as a secretary and in hotel management, until, eventually, a catastrophic event took matters out of her hands.

In an ironic twist of fate, unusually heavy rainfall caused the Squitter Brook to infiltrate otherwise solid foundations and flood the cellar and ground-floor rooms of Lower Mill; much as the waters under the earth invaded Doddington Manor in *The Waters Under the Earth*. John Moore's library and archive suffered badly; two thousand letters from all manner of celebrities, two hundred valuable books and several of his annual journals were destroyed. The insurance company paid for repairs to the house and fabric, but the experience shattered Lucile's resolve and she sold up. Afterwards she lived comfortably in smaller accommodation in the nearby village of Overbury, before finding happiness in a second marriage to Arthur Bell, a retired headmaster. Following his death in 1996, she moved from their home to live alone in a small cottage tucked away behind one of Tewkesbury's busy streets and within easy walking distance of the Abbey.

Lucile died in 2003, having devoted her last years ensuring that John Moore's name and work endures. She persuaded the people of Tewkesbury to remember him in several ways. The John Moore Countryside Museum, housed in one of those medieval Abbey cottages he did so much to save, commemorates him as naturalist and conservationist. There is a school named after him and his fictional place name – Elmbury – is immortalised on road signs and buildings. Tourists pass along a way-marked route between those places featured in his stories: Tudor House, The Abbey, The Uplands, Moore & Sons, Abel Fletcher's Mill, the Swan Hotel and Grammar School. He is remembered annually at the Cheltenham Festival of Literature by a distinguished literary figure or conservationist delivering a John Moore lecture and The John Moore Society ensures that his books, journalism and broadcasting are available to an ever-increasing number of enthusiasts.

And, for all his desire to be recognised as a famous novelist, John Moore would be more than content with the knowledge that he is best remembered as a true countryman, and by his peers as a thoroughly decent chap.

David Cole
Inkberrow

Personal Profiles

Sir Kingsley William AMIS (1922-95). English novelist, poet, critic and teacher. Author of many novels, including *Lucky Jim* and *The Old Devils.* Served Second World War in Royal Signals. Educated Oxford University. Lecturer in English at University of Wales 1948-61 & Cambridge University 1961-3. Father of novelist Martin Amis.

Dame Edith Margaret Emily 'Peggy' ASHCROFT (1907-91). Best known as a classical stage actress, but also significant appearances on film and television – most notably as Mrs Moore in *A Passage to India* and Barbie Batchelor in *The Jewel in the Crown,* for both of which she received awards.

Herbert Ernest 'H.E.'BATES CBE (1905-74). Prolific author of more than 60 books. Began his working life as a journalist in his native Northamptonshire, the setting for his early works. Commissioned into the RAF in the Second World War he wrote about his experiences under the pseudonym 'Flying Officer X'. Best remembered for *Fair Stood the Wind for France, The Purple Plain, Uncle Silas* and *The Darling Buds of May.*

Sir John BETJEMAN (1906-84). English poet, writer and broadcaster. Much loved eccentric who described himself as incurably indolent. His ability to write popular poetry and an interest in architecture combined to support him throughout life. Began life as a lowly journalist after failing to graduate from Oxford University and rose to become Poet Laureate in 1972.

Gordon BOTTOMLEY (1874-1948). Yorkshire-born author, poet and playwright. Friend of poet Edward Thomas.

Ivor BROWN (1891-1974). Critic, journalist, essayist and novelist. Recognised for a 'commonsensical' view of literature and life, and for his books about the English language.

Sir Arthur BRYANT (1899-1985). Author and history lecturer at Oxford University. Held notoriously trenchant right-wing opinions.

John BUCHAN (1st Baron TWEEDSMUIR) (1875-1940). Scottish-born and Oxford-educated. One of the most successful popular novelists of his day, possessed of a genius for friendship Also a biographer and politician – Governor General of Canada from 1935 until his death. Writer of more than 80 books, including *Prester John* and *The Thirty-Nine Steps.*

Dame Barbara CARTLAND (1901-2000). Educated Malvern Girls' College. Romantic novelist credited with 724 titles. First worked as a journalist and gossip columnist. Father killed in First World War – 2 brothers killed within a day of each other while serving at Dunkirk in 1940.

Ronald CARTLAND (1907-40). Brother of above. Unionist Member of Parliament for a Birmingham constituency 1935-40. Volunteered for military service in 1939, prior to outbreak of Second World War. Killed at Dunkirk.

Lord Edward Christian David Gascoyne CECIL (1902-86). Aristocrat, literary scholar, teacher and writer of criticism and biography (including Jane Austen and Lord Melbourne). Professor of English Literature, New College, Oxford University 1948-69.

Richard CHURCH (1893-1972). A Londoner who followed a career as a civil servant for 30 years, before becoming an editor at Dents' publishing house where he looked after the young John Moore. A respected writer, poet and critic in his own right. Published three well-received volumes of autobiography.

William COBBETT (1763-1835). Traveller, adventurer, soldier, who became a radical agriculturalist and prolific journalist. Campaigned for the 1832 Reform Act. *Rural Rides*, published 1830, is his enduring legacy to understanding the conditions of the time.

Sir William Alexander Roy COLLINS (1900-76). Educated Harrow and Oxford University. Member of publishing dynasty. Chairman and Managing Director, William Collins Ltd, publishers of the majority of John Moore's post-war books.

Neil Michael DAUNT, OBE (1909-90). Failed to complete engineering degree at Cambridge University because of an obsession for flying. Joined RAF and became a member of its aerobatic team. Leaving to become a test-pilot, he flew the prototype jet-propelled aircraft, the Gloster-Whittle, and its successor the Meteor – a twin-engine fighter that entered operational service in 1943. A flamboyant larger-than-life *bon vivant*, he subsequently followed careers as farmer, salesman and chief technician of a hospital's kidney unit. Daunt married three times and John Moore was Godfather to his eldest son, whose birth he announced in a telegram as 'Beezlebub has landed'.

Norman EDWARDS, journalist. Employed by Amalgamated Press. Member of the Savile Club, where he met John Moore. Editor of *TV Mirror*, afterwards becoming editor of *Everybody's Magazine* in 1956 and then a freelance writer.

Cecil Scott 'C.S.'FORESTER, born Cecil Louis Troughton Smith in Cairo (1899-1966). Educated Dulwich College. Studied medicine before becoming a writer following the successful publication of his first novel in 1926. Wrote the later filmed *African Queen* in 1935 and created Horatio Hornblower for the eleven-book series of maritime conflict during the Napoleonic period. Suffered ill-health and moved to the USA during the Second World War, where his propaganda output was credited with helping to secure support for Britain before America's actual involvement in the conflict.

Christopher FRY, born Christopher Harris (1907-2005). English playwright who shot to fame in the 1940s with *The Lady's Not for Burning* and *Venus Observed* both conveying an optimism about humanity and a sense of divine providence that the public found consoling after years of war. Had the unenviable distinction of being often bottom of his form at school, but this did not deter his precocious talent as a poet and dramatist, completing his first full-length verse play at 14. Before full-time writing he taught at a prep school, as an administrator for Dr Barnardo and as a stage director. After many years of frantic creativity he lost confidence and turned to play translation and film scripts. Later he wrote prodigiously for television.

John Wilton HAINES (1875-1960). A Gloucester solicitor with a reputation as a poet and naturalist, who counted among his friends all the foremost poets of his day. He and his wife were keen botanists who spent much time in the Forest of Dean of which he served as a Verderer until his death.

Gilbert Charles HARDING (1907-60). Born Hereford. On death of father educated Royal Orphanage, Wolverhampton and Cambridge University. Variously journalist, schoolmaster, police officer, disc-jockey, radio and TV personality (Twenty Questions and What's My Line). A reputation as the rudest man in Britain.

Colonel Robert Quixano HENRIQUES (1905-67). Soldier, writer, landowner and farmer. Educated Rugby and Oxford University. Commissioned into Royal Artillery 1926, but retired in 1933 to write. He served with the army commando services throughout the Second World War, reaching the rank of Colonel, afterwards farming in Gloucestershire. Wrote several books and was co-chairman with John Moore of Cheltenham Literary Festival for some years.

Robert 'Parson' HERRICK (1591-1674). A London-born priest and poet who wrote his best work during a 31 year ministry at a secluded rural parish in Devon. Noted for a bawdy style and is probably best remembered for the line – 'gather ye rosebuds while ye may'.

Elizabeth Jane HOWARD (born 1923), English novelist. Former actress and model. Prize-winning first novel, 1951 – *The Beautiful Visit.* Best known for four-part family saga, later televised as *The Cazalets.* Married first to Sir Peter Scott, the naturalist and wild-life artist, and thirdly to author Sir Kingsley Amis.

Paul HUMPHREYS (1913-2003). Born Paris. Educated London. Journalist and industrialist before entering BBC during Second World War. Features editor and writer before becoming Talks Editor of Midland region. Recruited John Moore for post-war broadcasts.

Major General Walter Morland HUTTON CB, DSO, MC* (1912-94). Commissioned from RMA Sandhurst into Royal Tank Corps, 1932. Awarded first MC Palestine 1936. Second World War, fought through North Africa (including Alemein) and Italy. Awarded DSO and second MC. Commandant, Sandhurst 1944-5. Remained in Army until 1966, when he became Bursar of Jesus College, Oxford. 'Jimmy' Hutton was romantically involved with Lucile before she met John Moore.

Andrew Leicester IRVINE (1881-1967). Educated Winchester and Oxford University. A noted Classical scholar. Sixth-form teacher and housemaster at Charterhouse from 1914 to retirement in 1946. Spent his retirement as a publisher's proof-reader.

George Colin JACKSON (1921-81). Born Tewkesbury. Educated Tewkesbury Grammar School and Oxford University. Barrister, lecturer, writer and broadcaster. African and Middle-East foreign affairs specialist. Labour Member of Parliament for the Brighouse and Spenborough constituency 1964-70 and 1974-9.

Amy JOHNSON (1903-41). English Aviatrix who graduated from Sheffield University and obtained a pilot's licence in 1929. A year later she became the first woman to fly solo from the United Kingdom to Australia, for which she was awarded the CBE. Went on to undertake other record-breaking flights before joining the Air Transport Auxiliary in 1940 as a ferry pilot. She was forced to bail out of an aircraft over London in 1941 and her body was never found.

Sir Ludovic Henry Coverley KENNEDY (born 1919). Educated Oxford University. Campaigning investigative reporter, author, television journalist and news reader. Served Second World War in destroyers and at the Admiralty Press Division. Married the actress and dancer Moira Shearer in 1950; John Moore was godfather to their eldest child.

Captain Anthony KIMMINS OBE RN (retd) (1901-64). Educated RN – Osborne and Dartmouth. Served First World War, retiring in 1932 to become author, playwright, film producer and director. Second World War – recalled for duties with naval intelligence and information in various theatres of the war.

Marghanita LASKI (1915-88). English journalist, novelist, biographer, playwright and popular broadcaster (What's My Line). Educated Oxford University.

John LAURIE (1897-1980). Scottish Shakespearean actor who also became well known for his portrayal of Private Fraser in the television series, 'Dad's Army'. Several film appearances.

Laurie LEE (1914-97). Gloucestershire poet and novelist originating from humble beginnings in Slad Valley, Stroud. Second World War – GPO film unit as a scriptwriter. Best known for *Cider With Rosie* (1959).

Cecil Day LEWIS (1904-72). English poet. Educated Oxford University. First met John Moore when employed as a schoolmaster and engaged in the anti-fascist movement in the 1930s. Wrote crime novels under the pen-name Nicholas Blake to supplement income. Second World War – employed in Ministry of Information. Later Professor of Poetry, Oxford University, and appointed Poet Laureate, 1968.

Eric Robert Russell LINKLATER (1899-1974). Novelist and travel writer. Served First World War in rank of major and Second World War at War Office.

Sir Edward Montague Compton 'Monty' MACKENZIE (1883-1972). Scottish writer and novelist who produced over a hundred books. Best known for *Whisky Galore* and *Monarch of the Glen.* Served in British Intelligence during First World War. Early radio personality and one of television's first big names. Is credited with leading a colourful life and being a passionate advocate for Scottish independence. John Moore's greatest friend and supporter.

Wolf MANKOWITZ (1924-98). One of Britain's most prolific post-war playwrights, screen-writer and novelist. Educated Cambridge University. Wrote screenplays A Kid for Two Farthings, The Millionairess, Casino Royale, Black Beauty and Expresso Bongo.

Sir John MASEFIELD (1878-1967). English poet and writer. Poet Laureate 1930-67. Born Ledbury, Herefordshire. Educated Warwick School and HMS *Conway.* Merchant Navy officer and spent time as a hobo in USA, returning home in 1897 to write. Served as a medical orderly on the Western Front throughout First World War.

André MAUROIS (1885-1967). French author and man of letters. First World War – liaison officer with British Army and thereafter a committed anglophile. Wrote popular book of experiences, *The Silence of Colonel Bramble.* Served Second World War in Free French Army. Long career as biographer, historical writer and author of children's books.

Nicholas John Turney MONSARRAT (1910-79). Educated Winchester and Cambridge University. Abandoned law studies to become a writer. Served with distinction in convoy escorts with Royal Navy in Second World War and latterly in Admiralty Press Division. Entered Diplomatic Service after the war, serving in South Africa and Canada. Best remembered for sea stories (*The Cruel Sea*) and wrote fulltime from 1959.

MOORE family:

Dr George MOORE (1808-89). John Moore's great-grandfather. London surgeon who was persuaded to return to the county of his birth by a wealthy patient (Samuel Warneford – see below). Set up practice at Moreton-in-Marsh. Fathered 14 children from two marriages; one of whom was

Dr John New MOORE JP, MRCS, LSA (1840-1904). John Moore's grandfather. Surgeon qualified at St Mary's Hospital, London. Worked as ship's surgeon on Peninsular and Oriental Lines before joining his father's practice. Together with wife, Shirley, indulged a passion for fox-hunting, eventually employing assistants to run his practice and thereby disposing of the considerable legacy left by his father. His marriage produced two daughters, one of whom was Georgina Eliza (Ina) MOORE (1873-1958) John Moore's mother, who in 1905 had married her cousin

Cecil Charles MOORE (1861-1918). Grandson of Dr George Moore's elder brother, William. Junior partner in Tewkesbury firm of Moore & Sons. Inland Revenue Commissioner, Justice of the Peace, local politician, Mayor and Alderman.

Daphne Mary MOORE (1910-2004). John Moore's sister. Inherited the family's hunting gene and devoted her life to the chase. For many years she was hunting correspondent of *Horse and Hound* and wrote several authoritative books on the subject. Following the death of her mother in 1958 she lived at Badminton under the patronage of the Duke and Duchess of Beaufort, within sound of the famous kennels; she became an internationally renowned expert on hound bloodlines and pedigrees. In great old age, she moved to a residential home, where her greatest loss was singing hounds greeting each new dawn.

Blanche Penelope Turner, née MOORE (1850-1943). The infamous red-haired 'Aunt Paddy'. A sister of Dr. John Moore who married Arthur Turner, Medical Officer of Health at Tewkesbury. Possessed of notorious temper, becoming the family matriarch of whom everyone walked in fear. The matchmaker between Ina and Cecil Moore.

Thomas Weaver MOORE (1855-1938). Elder brother of Cecil and senior partner in family firm. Justice of the Peace, local politician, Mayor and alderman. Pillar of the Tewkesbury Abbey community. His family of seven children included two sons, both of whom died in France during the First World War – Harold, aged 32 years, was already a partner in the business when he volunteered to serve and Lionel, 23, interrupted his fourth-year medical studies at Guy's Hospital, London.

Neville MOORE (1869-1941). 'Uncle Jim', brother of Thomas and Cecil. Tewkesbury solicitor and HM Coroner (1900-34). Once described by his niece Daphne as the most glum man in England which, given his occupation, may be of little surprise. Father of

Denis Neville MOORE (1910-2003). John Moore's cousin who accompanied him to boarding school. Denis was a prodigious sporting talent, particularly at cricket. Educated Shrewsbury and Oxford University. Captain of Oxford, 1931. Scored 206 on debut for Gloucestershire. Illness curtailed any progress to international honours and he thereafter concentrated his efforts towards a successful career in the law.

William Shepherd 'Shakes' MORRISON, (lst Viscount DUNROSSIL) (1893-1961). Educated Edinburgh University. Awarded Military Cross – First World War. Member of Parliament for Cirencester and Tewkesbury from 1929. Long ministerial career. Speaker of House of Commons 1951-9. Governor General of Australia 1960.

John Gerald O'BRIEN (1889-1958). New Zealand farmer who took exception to passage about the Irish in *Portrait of Elmbury.* Fought with New Zealand Army in both World Wars. An international rugby player who features in the All-Black Hall of Fame. A renowned full-back whose career was affected by the First World War, but nevertheless represented his country on 12 occasions. He was described as a master of positional play to the point of wizardry and Edward, Prince of Wales, once said of him, 'If I dropped a kitbag from the dome of St Paul's, O'Brien would surely catch it'.

Eric PARKER (1870-1955). Educated Eton and Oxford University. Shooting Editor of *The Field*, 1911-37, General Editor, 1930-7 and of *The Lonsdale Library*. Author of many publications associated with sport and rural matters.

Eric PARTRIDGE (1894-1979). Noted English language lexicographer. Born New Zealand. Settled in England after First World War army service, becoming a travelling Oxford University fellow. Schoolteacher and from 1927 a full-time writer, working from the same desk at the British Library every day. Author of more than forty books.

Augustus Dudley PETERS (1892-1973). Educated Cambridge University. Literary agent and theatre producer. Second World War – head of public relations, Ministry of Food.

John Boynton PRIESTLEY OM (18941984). After serving in – France during First World War studied at Cambridge University on an officer's discharge grant before establishing himself as a significant author and dramatist. Well known for *The Good Companions* and *An Inspector Calls,* among more than 120 publications and plays.

Sir Ralph David RICHARDSON (1902-83). Born Cheltenham. Second World War Fleet Air Arm pilot. English actor and theatrical knight. Primarily a stage career as a star of the Old Vic theatre and Royal Shakespeare Company, but also select television and film appearances.

John William ROBERTSON SCOTT CH, MA (1866-1962). Traveller, author, newspaper editor; latterly founder and editor for 21 years of *The Countryman Magazine.* Activist for abolition of cruel sports who listed his outdoor leisure pursuits as anything except hunting, shooting, fishing and racing.

Raymond SAVAGE (died 1964). Managing Director, RS Ltd, Literary Agency, 1924-47. Director and literary adviser Evans Bros Ltd, 1947-50.

George Bernard SHAW (1856-1950). Born Dublin. Radical socialist and reformer. Began journalism career as a music critic, before becoming a prolific author and playwright. Wrote acclaimed works *Pygmalion* and *Saint Joan.*

George SHERINGHAM (1884-1937). Son of Vicar of Tewkesbury. Educated King's School, Gloucester and the Slade School of Art. Artist, writer, illustrator, stage and costume designer.

Hugh Tempest SHERINGHAM (1876-1930). Brother of above. Educated Westminster and Cambridge University. Author and Angling Editor of *The Field*, 1903-30.

Emma SMITH (born 1923) . In Second World War volunteered for work on canals as a boatwoman and rose to fame in the late 1940s with a best-selling novel based upon the experience – *Maidens' Trip*. After travelling to India with a film unit she wrote another – *The Far Cry* – before fading away into obscurity when widowed and with two young children to care for. A friend of Laurie Lee, credited with encouraging him to complete his own best-seller *Cider with Rosie*. *The Far Cry* was republished in 2002.

Charles Percy 'C.P.'SNOW, The Baron Snow of Leicester (1905-80). Educated Leicester and Cambridge Universities. Physicist and author. Government technical director. Original scientific thinker, but best remembered for sequence of political novels under the collective title of *Strangers and Brothers.*

Eric Sherwood de Butts TAVERNER (1892-1958). Educated Winchester and Oxford University. In the first flight of angling authors and undoubtedly one of the most important contributors to sporting knowledge of his generation. Responsible for many classic volumes, including those on salmon and trout for the Lonsdale Library, and a prolific writer for periodicals, he still enjoys an international reputation fifty years after his death.

Dylan Marlais THOMAS (1914-53). Welsh poet and writer. One of the most exciting 20th century poets in the English language, and also one of the greatest. Noted for radio play *Under Milk Wood* and best remembered and quoted poems 'Do not go Gentle into that Good Night' and 'Death shall have no Dominion'.

Brian Percy Seymour VESEY-FITZGERALD (1900-81). Educated Oxford University. Authority on working animals, dogs, cats, nature, rural affairs and a prolific author. A supporter and spokesman for the Romany gypsy. Popular broadcaster, mainly as an interpreter of and commentator on the countryside. Editor of *The Field* 1940-5. Once wrote to John Moore: 'We seem to have two J.C. Moores – which are you – one wrote *The Countryman's England*, which I think is the best book of its type I have ever read'.

Samuel Wilson WARNEFORD (1763-1855). Educated Oxford University. Wealthy clergyman; one-time parson at Bourton-on-the-Hill, near Moreton-in-Marsh, who persuaded Dr George Moore to give up his London practice and return to the Cotswolds. Was a generous benefactor, giving over £200,000 to various causes during his lifetime (founder of Leamington Hospital, medical scholarship at King's College, London University, legacy to Queen's Hospital, Birmingham, and Clergy Orphans' school, etc.). On death, left his large family home and a substantial sum of money to Dr George Moore.

Terence Hanbury 'Tim' WHITE (1906-64). Educated Cambridge University. First employed as a master at Stowe School where he began to write. An intensely involved amateur naturalist with interests in hunting, fishing and hawking. Wrote a moving account of his unsuccessful attempt to train a wild hawk – *The Goshawk* – but is better known for a sequence of Arthurian novels. The film *Camelot* was based upon his *The Once and Future King* and earned his fortune. His life was destroyed by alcohol.

Francis Brett YOUNG (1884-1954). Popular English novelist and poet who firstly qualified in medicine from Birmingham University. During First World War served in France as a major with Medical Corps until invalided out, after which he did not again practice medicine. Became a full-time writer from 1927 and was responsible for numerous books, including *My Brother Jonathan*, *Portrait of a Village*, *Far Forest*, *Dr Bradley Remembers* and *A Man about the House.*

Notes

Abbreviations - PofE (*Portrait of Elmbury*, London: Collins, 1945); BMCC (*Birmingham Mail* Country Column); FAA (Fleet Air Arm); RNAS (Royal Naval Air Station); RNAH (Royal Naval Auxillary Hospital); JM (John Moore); EGM (Eliza Georgina [Ina] Moore, mother); L (Lucile, wife); DMM (Daphne Mary Moore, sister)

Introduction.

1. *The Boys' Country Book*, London: Collins, 1961.

Chapter 1

1. PofE.
2. PofE.
3. From reminiscences by DMM.
4. PofE.
5. PofE.
6. PofE.
7. PofE.
8. PofE.
9. From article, 'Tewkesbury Abbey' by JM, publisher unknown.
10. As above.
11. As above.
12. As above.
13. PofE.
14. From *Rural Rides* by William Cobbett.
15. From *Pickwick Papers* by Charles Dickens.
16. From notes for an address to Tewkesbury Civic Society, 1952.
17. As above.
18. As above.
19. As above.

20. BMCC, 1954.
21. BMCC, 1954.
22. From article, 'An Arcadian Sunlight' by JM, publisher unknown.
23. PofE.
24. From article, 'Memories of a Butterfly Hunter' by JM, *Country Life Annual*, 1964.
25. PofE.
26. PofE.
27. JM to an unknown correspondent, 1936.
28. JM's Nature Notes, c.1920
29. PofE.
30. PofE.
31. PofE.
32. From article published in *Lilliput* magazine, April 1958.
33. PofE.
34. *Malvern News*, 24 November 1923.
35. PofE.

Chapter 2.

1. PofE.
2. Archive material.
3. As above.
4. As above.
5. As above.
6. *Malvern Gazette*, 23 May 1924.
7. PofE.
8. JM Journal, c.1929.
9. PofE.
10. From article, 'Distress' by JM, *Gloucestershire Countryside* magazine, 1 November 1931.
11. Reverend Ernest Smith, vicar of Tewkesbury, 16 April 1930.
12. PofE.
13. PofE.
14. PofE.
15. *Cheltenham Chronicle* 1930.

16. PofE.
17. Archive material.
18. John Wilton Haines, solicitor, poet and critic, 1935.
19. As above.
20. As above.
21. *The Field* magazine, 1929.
22. JM Journal, c.1930.
23. DMM in conversation with author, 2002.
24. *Country Life* magazine, 1929: 'A Memory of Otter Hounds'.
25. JM Journal, c.1929.
26. *Hutchins Magazine*, date unknown.
27. A.E. Clifford, relationship and date unknown.
28. Barbara Cartland, author and friend, 1929.
29. *Dixon's Cubs*, London: Dent, 1930.
30. *Boston Transcript*, 15 May 1930.

Chapter 3

1. *Tewkesbury Register & Gazette*, February/March 1931.
2. As above.
3. As above.
4. As above.
5. As above.
6. From an article, 'A Tilt at Bloomsbury' by JM 1932, publication unknown
7. As above.
8. Editorial note by JM, *The Book of the Fly Rod*, London: Eyre & Spottiswoode, 1936.
9. *Tramping Through Wales*, London: Dent, 1931.
10. Letter from unidentified correspondent, 12 November 1931.
11. *Tramping Through Wales*, London: Dent, 1931.
12. JM, 1951 (biographical note for *Woman's Own* magazine).
13. JM to EGM, 1938 (London).
14. From a series of letters from JM to EGM, March/April, 1932 (Spanish journey).
15. As above.
16. As above.

17. As above.
18. As above.
19. Lecture notes April, 1937 (Anti-Fascist Rally, Cheltenham Town Hall).
20. Letter from Richard Church, author and editor at Dents, 1932.
21. *Cheltenham Chronicle*, 12 December 1931.
22. Eric Taverner, writer and author, 1933.
23. As above.
24. John Wilton Haines, personal comment, 1933.
25. John Wilton Haines, as a reviewer, 1933, (publication unknown).
26. *The Welsh Marches*, London: Chapman & Hall, 1933.
27. *The New Forest*, London: Chapman & Hall, 1936.
28. As above.
29. *The Cotswolds*, London: Chapman & Hall, 1937.
30. As above.
31. *A Walk Through Surrey*, London: Chapman & Hall, 1939.
32. As above.
33. JM to EGM, 1938 (London).
34. 'The Tower' by JM, *Homes & Gardens*, 1963.
35. As above.
36. Churchwardens' Accounts, Tewkesbury Abbey, 1593.
37. *Tewkesbury Register & Gazette*, 1935.
38. As above.
39. As above.
40. Phylis Peregrine in conversation with author, 2002.
41. JM to Constance Babbington Smith, author, 1965.
42. Squadron Leader Orlebar, Commanding Officer, RAF Northolt, 1939.
43. JM to EGM, 1937 (London).
44. JM to EGM, 1937 (London).
45. JM to EGM,1937 (London).
46. JM to EGM, 1937 (London).
47. JM to EGM, 1937 (London).
48. JM to EGM, 1937 (London).

49. JM to EGM, 1937 (London).
50. JM to EGM, 1937 (High Wycombe).
51. JM to EGM, 1937 (High Wycombe).
52. JM to EGM, 1940 (RNAS, Eastleigh).
53. *The Countryman's England*, London: Seeley Service, 1939.
54. JM to Mrs Pouncey, wife of the vicar of Tewkesbury, 1962.

Chapter 4

1. JM to EGM, 1939 (RNAS, Eastleigh).
2. JM to EGM, 1939 (RNAS, Eastleigh).
3. JM to EGM, 1939 (RNAS, Eastleigh).
4. JM to EGM, 1939 (RNAS, Eastleigh).
5. JM to EGM, 1940 (RNAS, Eastleigh).
6. JM to EGM, 1940 (RNAS, Eastleigh).
7. JM to EGM, 1940 (RNAS, Eastleigh).
8. JM to Elizabeth Kluer, poet and friend, 1940 (RNAS, Eastleigh).
9. JM to EGM, 1940 (RNAS, Eastleigh).
10. FAA signal Fleet Air Arm Records.
11. JM to John Wilton Haines, 1940 (RNAS, Ford).
12. JM to EGM, 1940 (RNAS, Ford).
13. JM to EGM, 1940 (RNAS, Ford).
14. JM to EGM, 1940 (RNAS, Ford).
15. JM to EGM, 1940 (RNAS, Ford).
16. BMCC, 2 September 1949.
17. JM to EGM, 1942 (RAF, Duxford).
18. JM to EGM, 1940 (RNAS, Arbroath).
19. JM to EGM, 1941 (RNAH, Kirriemuir).
20. JM to EGM, 1941 (USA).
21. JM to EGM, 1941 (USA).
22. Personal journal note, 1941.
23. As above.
24. As above.
25. As above.
26. FAA signal – Fleet Air Arm Records.
27. JM, personal journal note, 1941.

28. As above.
29. As above.
30. Telegram to EGM, 17 October 1941, from RNAH, Barrow Gurney, Bristol.
31. JM to EGM, 1941 (RNAH, Barrow Gurney).
32. JM to EGM, 1942 (RAF, Duxford).
33. E.F. Bosman, editor, Dents, 1942.
34. T.J. Morrison, film editor, 1942.
35. JM to EGM, 1942 (RNAH, Barrow Gurney).
36. JM to EGM, 1942 (RAF, Duxford).
37. JM to EGM, 1942 (Press Division, the Admiralty, London).
38. JM to EGM, 1942 (Press Division, the Admiralty, London).
39. JM to EGM. 1942 (Press Division, the Admiralty, London).
40. Sir Compton Mackenzie, *My Life & Times*, London: Chatto & Windus, 1968.
41. JM to EGM, 1942 (London).
42. Sir Compton Mackenzie, *My Life and Times*, see note 40.
43. JM to EGM, 1943 (HMS *Tracker*).
44. JM to EGM, 1943 (Glasgow).
45. JM to EGM, 1944 (Press Division, the Admiralty, London).
46. 'The Story of the Berries' by JM, from RN Records (Historical Branch), not published.
47. 'Sonnet For Dead Comrades' by JM, published in *Wavy Navy*, London: Harrap, 1950.
48. JM to Gordon Bottomley, author, 1943.
49. 'Forts Going Out' by JM, 1943, publishers various.
50. JM to EGM, 1943 (London).
51. JM to Michael Daunt, test pilot and friend, 1944 (London).
52. JM to L, 1944 (London).
53. JM to EGM, 1944 (London).
54. JM to EGM, 1941 (RNAS, Sandbanks).
55. JM to EGM, 1943 (London).
56. JM to EGM, 1944 (London).
57. JM to EGM, 1944 (London).
58. JM to EGM, 1944 (London).
59. EGM to JM, 1944 (Tewkesbury).

60. JM to EGM, 1944 (secret location, Hampshire).
61. JM to EGM, 1 June 1944 (Portsmouth).
62. JM, personal journal, 1944.
63. As above.
64. As above.
65. As above.
66. L in conversation with author, 2001.
67. JM to EGM, 1944 (London).
68. JM to EGM, 1944 (London).

Chapter 5

1. JM to TH White, friend and author, 1945.
2. PofE.
3. JM to John Wilton Haines, as a friend, 1945.
4. PofE.
5. JM, personal journal, 1946.
6. PofE.
7. Thomas Moncrief, priest, to JM, 1946.
8. Stella Chapman, correspondent, to JM, 1947.
9. John Gerald O'Brien, correspondent, to JM, 1948.
10. As above.
11. From article by JM, 'The Homecoming', *Answers Magazine*, 1945.
12. As above.
13. JM, personal journal,1946.
14. As above.
15. *Brensham Village* by JM, London: Collins, 1946.
16. As above.
17. As above.
18. A.L. Irvine, retired Classics teacher and part-time proof-reader, to JM, 1947.
19. JM to A.L. Irvine, 1947.
20. From *Sixty Years at School* by A.L. Irvine, London: The Wykeham Press, 1958.
21. JM, personal journal, 1958.
22. Notes for article c 1951, publisher unknown.

23. BMCC, 1954.
24. *The Blue Field* by JM, London: Collins, 1948.
25. As above.
26. Torch Campbell, a correspondent, to JM, 1953.
27. From notes for speech at Dumbleton Cricket Club's Annual Dinner, date unknown.
28. BMCC, date unknown.
29. As above.
30. As above.
31. JM, notes for book reviews, 1952.
32. JM, notes for book review, 1951.
33. As above.
34. JM, notes for book review, 1950.
35. JM, notes for book review, 1952.
36. JM, personal journal, 1952.
37. JM to W. Bridges Adams, friend and retired theatre director, 1958.
38. As above.
39. BMCC, 1949.
40. Notes for Speech Day address, Tewkesbury High School, date unknown.
41. BMCC, 1964.
42. JM to editor, *Birmingham Mail*, 1964.
43. BMCC, 1953.
44. Reginald Gattward, Cheltenham Entertainment Services, to JM, 1953.
45. JM to Reginald Gattward, 1953.
46. BMCC, 1949.
47. JM, open letter, date and publication unknown.
48. BMCC, 1954.
49. *Birmingham Mail* letter pages, 1954.
50. BMCC, 1954.
51. BMCC, 1954.
52. Draft for BMCC, publication date unknown.
53. BMCC, date unknown.
54. BMCC, date unknown.

Chapter 6

1. JM, Introduction to 1953 Cheltenham Festival programme.
2. Notes for interval talk during Hill Players production, 1964.
3. Sidney Knight, writer and poet, to JM, 1954.
4. As above, 1960.
5. JM to Sidney Knight, 1954.
6. Sidney Knight to JM, 1959.
7. JM, notes for media publicity purposes, 1955.
8. JM to EGM, 1956.
9. JM to Michael Walter, editor at Collins, 1966.
10. JM to T.H. White, friend and author, 1954.
11. JM to Secretary, Herefordshire National Savings Committee, 1953.
12. JM, quoted in *Gloucestershire Echo*, 1953.
13. JM to EGM, 1953.
14. Inspector of Taxes to JM, 1953.
15. JM to Inspector of Taxes, 1954.
16. JM to A.D. Peters, literary agent, 1955.
17. BMCC, 1953.
18. JM to A.D. Peters, 1953
19. JM to T.H. White, 1959.
20. G. Griffiths, farmer, to JM, 1953.
21. J. Turner, farmer, to JM, 1953.
22. L. Farr, farmer, to JM, 1952.
23. J. Perry, farmer, to JM, 1952.
24. JM archive, draft document, date and intended recipient unknown.
25. JM to Barbara Cartland, friend and author, 1961.
26. *Truth* magazine, 1957, extract from review by Richard Church.

Chapter 7

1. JM, self-written publicity profile, 1966.
2. JM to Colin Jackson, friend, Member of Parliament, barrister and foreign correspondent 1964.
3. As above, 1960.

4. As above, 1966.
5. JM to Chief Constable, Gloucestershire Constabulary, 1957.
6. As above, 1959.
7. JM to editor, *The Times*, 1953.
8. JM to editor of unknown publication and date.
9. JM to Brian Purefoy, vicar, 1944.
10. JM to Chairman, Friends of Tewkesbury Abbey, 1952.
11. As above, 1953.
12. *Tewkesbury Register & Gazette*, 1967.
13. JM, *Tewkesbury Register & Gazette*, 1966.
14. As above, 1965.
15. As above, 1965.
16. As above, 1965.
17. As above.
18. JM, *Gloucestershire Echo*, 1965.
19. JM, aide memoir compiled for John Betjeman, 1965.
20. JM to Edward Stephens, schoolboy friend, 1959.
21. JM to A.D. Peters, literary agent, 1959.
22. From 'Words' by Edward Thomas.
23. *You English Words* by JM, London: Collins, 1961.
24. JM to Vice President, Esperanto Society, 1961.
25. From draft article for *Homes and Gardens* magazine, 1961.
26. BMCC 1962.
27. *Year of the Pigeons* by JM, London: Collins, 1963.
28. As above.
29. As above.
30. Nicholas Monsarrat, friend, wartime colleague and author, to JM, 1966.
31. JM personal journal, 1964.
32. *The Waters under the Earth* by JM, London: Collins, 1965.
33. JM, personal journal, 1964.
34. JM to A.D. Peters, 1965.
35. JM to A.D. Peters, 1967.
36. JM to DMM, 1967.
37. JM to Compton Mackenzie, friend and author, 1967.
38. L, diary entry, 1967.

39. JM to L, 1967.
40. Editor, *Birmingham Mail*, 28 July, 1967.
41. Tribute by Cosmo Pouncey, vicar of Tewkesbury, 1967.

Sequel

1. JM to Compton Mackenzie. 1967